The
SCRABBLE
Book

Derryn Hinch was born in New Zealand and has Scrabbled his way
through Canada, the United States and Australia where he is editor
of the *Sun* in Sydney.

Derryn Hinch

The

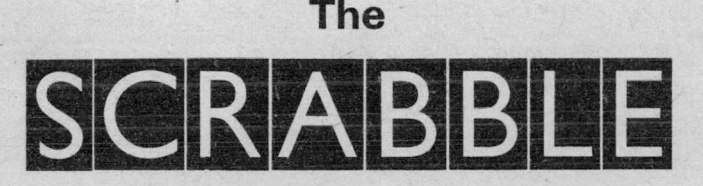

Book

Pan Books
in association with Macmillan London

For Eve
(even though her name is only worth
18 points on a triple-word square)

Revised British edition first published 1977 by Macmillan London Ltd
This edition published 1979 by Pan Books Ltd,
Cavaye Place, London SW10 9PG
in association with Macmillan London Ltd
© Derryn Hinch 1976, 1977
ISBN 0 330 25639 4
Printed and bound in Great Britain by
Richard Clay (The Chaucer Press) Ltd, Bungay, Suffolk

Quotation from *The Erection Set* by Mickey Spillane,
© Mickey Spillane 1972, reprinted by permission of the publishers,
E. P. Dutton & Co. Inc.

SCRABBLE R is the Registered Trade Mark owned in the United States
and Canada by Selchow and Righter Co., New York, in Australia by
Scrabble Australia Pty Ltd, and in most other countries by members
of the J. W. Spear & Sons Ltd, Enfield, Greater London Group.

Acknowledgment The publishers would like to thank Gyles Brandreth,
N.S.C. organizer, and J. W. Spear and Sons Ltd, for their help in preparing
the revised British edition, and Murfett Pty Ltd for their permission
to produce the book in Australia.

Contents

Part 4: Vocabulary

Acknowledgments

Thanks to the following people for their help in slaying the Jabberwock, for settling and sometimes inspiring Scrabble arguments, and for generally keeping my tiles straight in a manner that made this book possible:

My wife, Eve, for her nightly Scrabble games and for her marathon sessions immersed in dictionaries to help collate the diabolical lists of words used in this book.

My regular Scrabble opponents, Leonora Burton and Anthony Burton; Nancy Davis, my editor – and my first southpaw Scrabble freak; Estelle Hoffman for her secretarial help.

Britain's chief Scrabbler, Gyles Brandreth, for valuable aid on some distinctly British Scrabble traits.

The real Scrabble men, Alfred Butts and James Brunot, for their reminiscences and advice.

And my 88-year-old grandmother, Sarah Hinch, who was my first Scrabble opponent.

Sources

The following dictionaries were consulted as word authorities for the United Kingdom, Australian and New Zealand editions of this book:

The Oxford English Dictionary, Compact (1971) edition.
The Concise Oxford Dictionary, 1976 edition.

For the American edition the following dictionaries were used:

Webster's Third New International Dictionary (unabridged), 1971 edition.
Funk & Wagnalls Standard College Dictionary, 1973 edition.
The Random House Dictionary of the English Language (unabridged edition), 1967.

Introduction – Scrabble, the When and Why

Scrabble (skrab'el) *V.* **-bled, -bling,** *v.i.* 1. to scratch, scrape or paw, as with the hands. 2. To make irregular or meaningless marks; scribble. 3. To struggle or strive – *v.t.* 4. To make meaningless marks on; scribble on. 5. To gather hurriedly; scrape together. – *n.* 1. The act of scrabbling or scrambling. 2. A scrawling character mark, etc; scribble. 3. A sparse growth, as of underbrush. 4. The game of Scrabble.
Funk & Wagnalls Standard College Dictionary

Sophia Loren and Richard Burton did it to console him during one of his much-publicized estrangements from Elizabeth Taylor . . . Ageing madam Lucy Longstreet did it in a Mickey Spillane bestseller to warn the hero that he was walking into a trap . . . the Queen Mother admitted, back in 1954, that she was a novice at it . . . And out in New York's Brooklyn, middle-aged widow Frances Koestler does it by herself to cure her insomnia . . .

The thing that Sophia and Richard and Lucy and the Queen Mother and Frances have in common is a passion – a passion for a game called Scrabble.

More than 25 years since the game came on the market and well over 40 years since it was invented by an out-of-work American architect during the Depression, Scrabble has established itself as the most successful word game in history. In fact, this game, originally called Criss-crosswords by its inventor, Alfred Butts, has been elevated through its style and stratagems to the level of chess. These days anybody who used the words listed in a sample game in the lid of Scrabble sets would be annihilated. Words like *horn, farm, paste, mob* and *bit* have been replaced by such demons as *hajj*, *abaya*, *ilex*, *zloty* and *zoic*.

Now we have offensive Scrabble, and defensive Scrabble, and blocks and bluffs, and razor-edged stare-downs over challenged words that make poker hustlers look like a Sunday school class when it comes to honesty. The newest rage is Tournament Scrabble – a highly competitive, stopwatch version of the game, in which players have a maximum of two or three minutes in which to complete a turn. There are also Foreign Scrabble and Solitaire Scrabble.

Scrabble has been played on mountaintops and on safari in Africa. Nina Butts, wife of the inventor, tells a story of friends stumbling on a Scrabble game while on a tour of the Orient. 'Part of the trip took them through Japan,' she later told me. 'They climbed one of the mountains. I don't think it was Fuji-yama. Halfway up they saw two or three people resting by the side of the track. They were playing Scrabble.'

As mentioned earlier, Mickey Spillane used the game to save the life of the hero, Dogeron Kelly, in his novel *The Erection Set*. Spillane's thrillers have sold more than 50 million copies, which just about matches the number of Scrabble sets in circulation.

If Scrabble fans can get past the erotic picture of Spillane's naked wife on the cover and turn to page 269, they'll find Kelly about to walk into a killer's trap while former brothel-keeper Lucy Longstreet plays Solitaire Scrabble. As Spillane describes it:

> She was sitting by herself at a card table with a Scrabble game half-finished, an empty coffee cup beside her, looking as annoyed as hell.
>
> 'Lose your partner?' I asked her.
>
> 'Temporarily. Ain't much fun playing alone, so sit down, Johnny.'
>
> She reached her leg out under the table and kicked the chair out for me, squinted at me impatiently and said, 'Let me get this word down and you can play too.'

(Kelly was obviously a hot Scrabble player.)

There was something about her that wasn't hanging right, Spillane wrote, and when she picked up four tiles out of the holder and laid them down, it made a lousy job of Scrabble but a good piece of explanation. The word didn't fit, but it was clear enough. It spelled out T R A P (Kelly and Lucy Longstreet then hit the floor as the bullets started to fly, and Scrabble had saved a LIFE).

Frances Koestler of Brooklyn, who is now a Scrabble tournament player, says that Scrabble saved her life after her husband died eight years ago. 'We'd played Scrabble for years,' she told me. 'In fact, I was given one of the original sets of Criss-cross-words for a Christmas present back in 1943, and I've been playing ever since. Since my husband died, I've been an insomniac. But now I've learned to play Solitaire Scrabble. At night when I can't sleep, instead of having a beer, I'll play Solitaire for a couple of hours, and, do you know, I've trained myself not to let either hand cheat.'

Back during the Scrabble craze days of the 1950s it was considered very avant-garde to play 'smutty Scrabble' with four-letter words at parties — before the words were diverted to the cinema screen. And when the Queen Mother visited New York in 1954, *The New York Times* saw fit to print the fact that she bought a deluxe Scrabble set, complete with a revolving turntable.

Despite such royal interest, one of the major appeals of this game of mental gymnastics is that it is a game for everyone. For example, when the first British National Scrabble Championship was advertised in *The Times* in 1971, the organizer, Gyles Brandreth, received over 3,000 replies in four days, from people in all walks of life – from lorry drivers to aristocrats, from 10-year-olds to octogenarians. 'The one thing that all NSC participants seem to have in common,' comments Brandreth, 'is a passionate commitment to the game, sometimes a little too passionate for my liking! In the run up to the Finals one year, I was 'phoned by an anxious finalist at 4 o'clock one morning to be asked, "Is the word YEX allowed?"! (Yes, is the answer: it's a sort of hiccough).' Eventually the calls and queries became so numerous that Brandreth had to take his name out of the telephone directory and get the manufacturers of Scrabble to help with the correspondence.

The first American tournaments were organized in late 1973 and early 1974. In New York they had people ranging in age from 16 to 84 flocking to the Brooklyn War Memorial each Sunday where 2,000 contestants were whittled down to 50 finalists. Selchow & Righter, the company that now owns and manufactures Scrabble in the United States, hired a film crew to make a Scrabble documentary, and bosomy young women paraded around in T-shirts that spelled out SCRABBLE PLAYERS in game tiles on the front and that were so tight that the *B* tiles looked as though they should have been worth more than the legal three points.

Swept up in the new Scrabble-mania, four students in California set a world Scrabble marathon record of 100 hours that gained recognition in the *Guinness Book of Records*. Their record held for just over two years until in August 1975 four 'Down Under' Scrabble fanatics in Sydney, Australia, played non-stop in a shop window for 120 hours.

With Scrabble now in the top league, it's time for a complete book on the game, covering its strategy, history and aberrations. There are sections on how to play for fun, how to play for blood, how to score those lucrative seven-letter words that draw a fifty-point bonus, and how to improve your strategic vocabulary so that you always score between 400 and 600 points in a game. There are also chapters on Tournament Scrabble and on variations on the game, such as Blank (or Ecology) Scrabble – in which various letters, usually the blanks, are recycled during the game – and Unscrabble, which you play in reverse.

This book tells Scrabble fiends as well as Scrabble novices 'everything you've always wanted to know about Scrabble but didn't have the tiles to ask'. For example, did you know that there are dozens of two-letter words that are acceptable and that some championship players have memorized every one of them? They include good blocking words like *xi* and excellent hook words like *ai* and *ad*.

It will no doubt come as welcome news to many Scrabble players that they are in good company if they hate losing. I do. According to actor Richard Burton, the voluptuous Sophia Loren is a good Scrabble player but she detests losing. 'She's stupendously intelligent,' Burton said, after one game with the sultry Italian film star, 'but she can't bear to lose. You know she beat me twice . . . in English yet.'

The inventor of Scrabble, Alfred Butts, has a favourite story from the early days of his game. 'I was introduced to a woman as the inventor of Scrabble,' he recalled. 'She said, "Oh, is that so? My husband just loves it. I wish you'd tell me how to cook it."'

Few people nowadays are likely to confuse Scrabble – the world's most popular word game – with that American dish of fried pork scraps and meal called Scrapple. Actually, there is a vague connection. It was the food scrap days of the Depression that inspired the unemployed Butts to come up with an adult game which he hoped would make him rich. 'If there hadn't been any Depression in the Thirties there wouldn't be any Scrabble, I don't think.'

Butts was an out-of-work architect living in suburban New York, at the time. He was 34 years old, married, and – apart from his then unneeded talents as a designer – he had a passion for mind games.

He decided to invent one of his own.

Butts looked around at existing games on the market and analysed them. There were numbers games that used dice and cards, like bingo or housey-housey, and there were board games with men to be moved like draughts and chess. All of them seemed to be old. 'Putting men on a board started with draughts or chequers and finally led up to chess,' Butts said, 'and the numbers games started with dice. I believe the Egyptians had dice. Of course, in cards there was also bridge. It was still being improved in those days. There was bridge and auction bridge, and contract bridge was just coming out. Now when you say "bridge" there is just one game. But most of them were really old games. Mah-jongg was just an old Chinese game updated, and backgammon was having a comeback such as it had again in 1975. But backgammon was a combination of men on a board like draughts and the luck of a dice throw.'

Butts looked around and discovered that the other category of game was the word game. 'Playing with letters seemed to be the only other possibility, and there didn't seem to be anything but anagrams available.'

Architect Butts decided that would be the game upon which he would try to improve.

Game manufacturers were unanimously unimpressed with Butts' first game: a forerunner of Scrabble played with lettered tiles and racks but no board. His guinea pig friends and family liked it though and he kept working on refinements. 'I never lost faith in it. I knew there were the makings of something good there. I thought "Okay, the game companies don't like it as it is, I'll improve it."' He added a board . . . ordinary draught boards papered over with homemade blueprints. The game companies still didn't like the game. Most thought it was 'too highbrow' or 'too serious' or 'too complicated'. The manufacturers who rejected the game now rank alongside the film companies who thought *Gone With The Wind* was too long to be a commercial success.

The dogged development of Butts' Scrabble, and the repeated rejections from the manufacturers lasted from 1933 to 1938. In his basement, using a fretsaw and stick-on paper letters, Butts made about 50 sets of his game which then went under the name Criss-crosswords. He sold them at cost to friends. But commercially the game 'lay fallow' as Butts put it, until 1947 when an acquaintance looking for a 'quiet little business in the country' put a proposition to him.

The acquaintance, James Brunot, was just back from Washington where he had served as the wartime executive director of the President's War Relief and Control Board. Brunot resurrected Butts's game, changed the name to Scrabble, and by manufacturing the game himself (the game companies still weren't interested) he launched a phenomenon that *Look* magazine called 'the new parlormania'.

Alfred Butts with his trusty fretsaw had made 50 sets of his much-spurned game. Brunot would generate a business that produced more than fifty million sets of Scrabble in a word-game explosion that led *Life* magazine to comment in 1953 'no game in the history of the trade has ever sold so rapidly'.

So this is the game of Scrabble – played by widows alone and by film stars, jet-setters, lorry drivers, royalty, hustlers, writers, and indefatigable students. Dustin Hoffman plays it, and so did the Russian novelist Vladimir Nabokov. So did Nehru, and Oscar Hammerstein II. Madame Giscard d'Estaing, wife of the French president, plays it in French and in English and consistently wins in both languages.

I hope the following chapters will improve your Scrabble and settle the inevitable arguments that erupt around Scrabble tables everywhere.

I should point out that *scrabble* is a playable word, meaning 'to scratch, scrape or paw with the hands'. If you play it right and somehow stretch it through two triple-word squares, it can be worth 203 points.

A word of warning though: the word *scrabble* also means 'to make irregular or meaningless marks'.

Ah, I know the feeling well . . .

PART I
THE RULES OF THE GAME

1 What Is Scrabble – and How to Play It

Alfred Mosher Butts never knew what he was starting that Sunday morning over breakfast more than forty years ago when he said to his wife: 'Have a look at this when you've finished your breakfast . . . I think I've invented a new game.'

Anyone can play Scrabble.

Two seven-year-olds with a vocabulary no larger than *cat*, *mat*, *mum* and *dad* can have as much fun with the game as two English professors trying to outclass each other with words like *fuzil*, *mirza*, *zibet* and *zooid*. In special editions you can even play Scrabble if you speak only Russian or French or German. An Arabic edition has just arrived, and if you are blind you can play in braille.

If you have ever done a crossword in your life, then Scrabble is familiar territory (after all, it was first known as Criss-cross-words), and you are also prime Scrabble material if you have ever unjumbled an anagram or juggled with a cryptogram or deciphered one of those scrambled word games in the daily newspaper. When you boil it down, you are also good Scrabble material if you have ever played Happy Families or Snap or Ludo or Pin-the-Tail-on-the-Donkey or poker – or if you've ever read a book or owned a dictionary.

Once you start, you are involved in a game whose roots are in antiquity.

The game was not born until the 1930s, but Scrabble's inventor, Alfred Butts, concedes that the sport of deciphering anagrams had a big influence on him – and anagrams go back hundreds of years. The name *anagram* is derived from the ancient Greek *anagrammatismos*, which, admittedly, is a word you won't get much of a chance to use in Scrabble. At least it's proof, though, of just how old word games are.

The beauty of Scrabble is that the game incorporates the goals or styles of several different games. In a way it's like a crossword with each player trying to dovetail seemingly disparate letter combinations into complete words. It also has a hint of that popular old tile game called dominoes – because of the basic rule that no Scrabble tile can be played unless it can mate with a tile already on the board. There's more than a touch of poker's 'luck of the draw' when you face the uncertainty of drawing fresh tiles from the pool. And anyone who has unsuccessfully scanned the board for a place to attach a seven-letter word can immediately draw an analogy with Pin-the-Tail-on-the-Donkey.

So what is Scrabble? It's a mind game in which two, three or four players, using up to seven lettered tiles at a time, try to build words on a grid-pattern board. As props, you have 100 tiles with letters imprinted on them plus a board containing 225 squares for a playing surface.

Later in this book there are tips on how to play seven-letter bonus-scoring words, how to make strategic blocks and fades, how to manoeuvre your opponent out of high-scoring plays, and how to make judicious use of alleged problem letters. But none of these foreign-sounding things should scare a novice. Forget, at least for the moment, such things as the cut-throat tactics of Tournament Scrabble and the art of challenging, and forget the 'satire syndrome' and the 'polecat pass'. What you need first are the basics, and what follows here is a step-by-step breakdown on Scrabble for beginners.

As I said, anybody of any age and any educational background can play the game and enjoy it. It is true that good Scrabble players regularly score game totals in the high hundreds, and it is also true that two accomplished, highly competitive Scrabblers can expect to score 600 to 800 points between them in any game. Individually, a good Scrabble player should always score more than 300 points in a game, although a tight game, manipulated by a player skilled in the art of keeping the board 'tight', can inhibit the scoring. I have seen thrilling games played by two polished players where the scoring opportunities were so limited that the combined total just cleared 500.

The following is a scoring target so that you know how you are faring in a two-handed game. The scores are combined.

Beginners: 300–400
Average: 500–600
Good: 600–700
Professional: 700–800
Scrabble Champions: 800–?

Before you get discouraged by those high numbers, I should point out one basic Scrabble fact: It doesn't matter if you score only 150 points in a Scrabble game as long as your opponent scores only 149. That's all the game is about. You take the letters from the pool and place them across the grid board in such a way that they score more points than your opponent gets from his letter placement.

For reference purposes and for later recreation of good Scrabble moves, imagine your board is laid out something like a chess board with each square carrying a letter and a number for identification. The 15 horizontal squares are labelled from *A* to *O* (Board 1) with the letters running from left to right. The vertical squares are labelled from 1 to 15 from top to bottom. The key to this code, and an easy one to remember, is that if a word used is placed horizontally on the board, then the NUMBER is listed first. If the word is vertical, then the code LETTER is listed first.

Take, for example, the word *march* on Board 2. It is listed as 8 *F–J* because it starts on the eighth line and runs horizontally from the *F* square to the *J* square. The number is listed first to signal that the word is a horizontal one. If, instead, the word *march* were placed vertically on the board (Board 3) with the middle letter *R* still on the centre star, then it would be listed as *H* 6–10. The letter is listed first to signify a vertical word and

BOARD 1

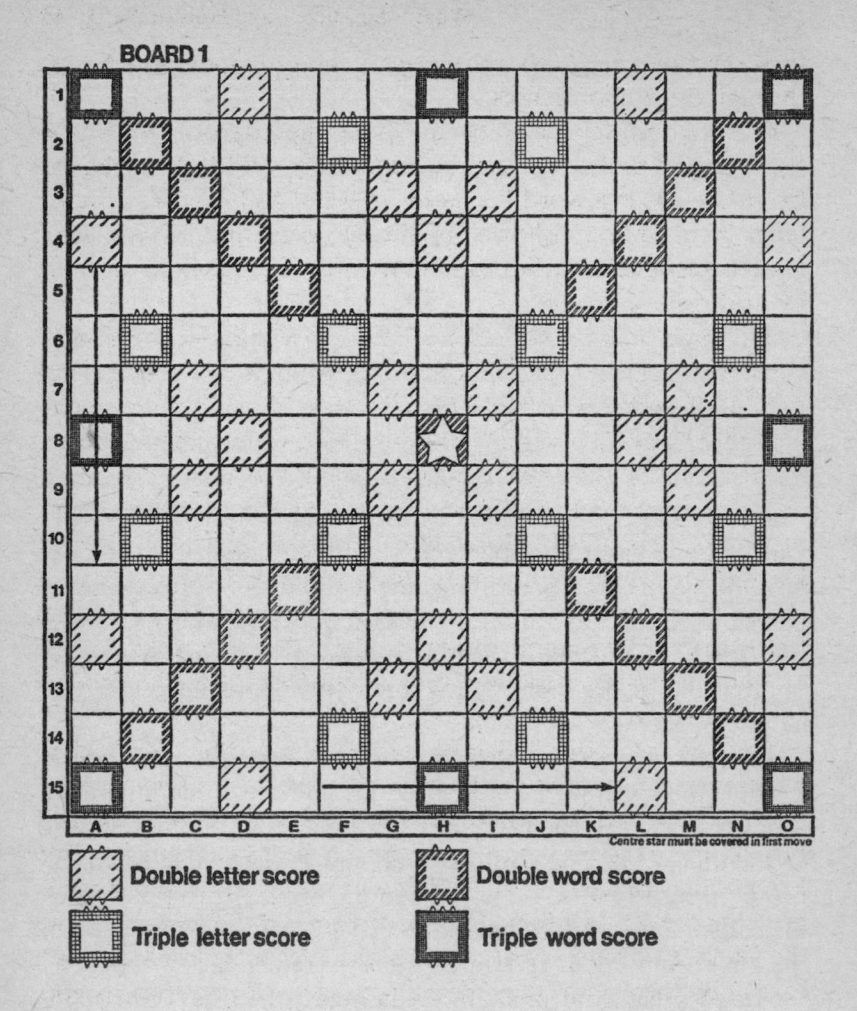

Centre star must be covered in first move

Double letter score

Triple letter score

Double word score

Triple word score

then the numbers 6–10 are given to show that the word runs through those coordinates.

The two things to remember are these: the letters run ACROSS the board from *A* to *O*, and the numbers run DOWN the board from 1 to 15. If a word is placed VERTICALLY, the constant letter is called first, followed by the numbers; and if it is placed HORIZONTALLY, the constant number is called first followed by the letters.

Although the idea for such a board configuration obviously comes from chess, I'll admit I first thought of it by remembering a childhood game we called Crush the Nazi Navy. It was a pencil-and-paper game – a variant of Battleships – in which the letters *c-r-u-s-h a-d-o-l-f* were written down one side of a sheet of paper and the numbers 1–10 were filled in along the bottom. Each player had one of those gridded paper oceans, and on it he hid his 'navy' by drawing lines of various lengths, signifying battleships. To score hits on your opponents' ships, you called out letter and number combinations, which he had to mark with a cross on his sheet. Any time the coordinates touched a hidden ship, you scored a 'hit'.

The hits you score in Scrabble are influenced by the number of letters you use in the words you make, the values of the letters you use to make them, and your placement of the tiles on the board, using the premium squares to collect extra points. The letter values range from a single point for an *E*, of which there are 12 in the set, to a high point of 10 each for the solitary *Z* and the single *Q*. There are also two blank tiles to be used as 'wild cards'. By themselves they have a face value of zero, but, as you will discover later, they are two of the most valuable tiles in the game. On the diagrammed boards in this book, blank tiles are always represented by heavy outline. The following is a list of all the letters in the alphabet plus their frequency in the Scrabble set and each letter's face value:

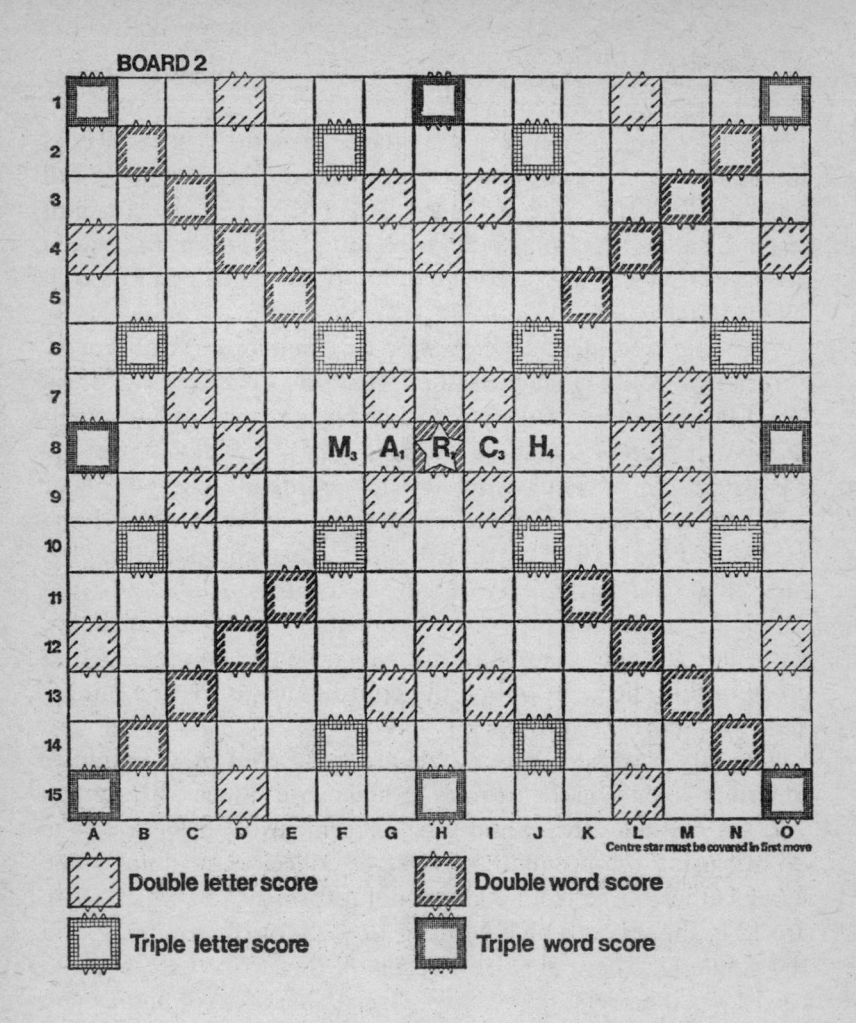

BOARD 2

Double letter score
Double word score
Triple letter score
Triple word score

Centre star must be covered in first move

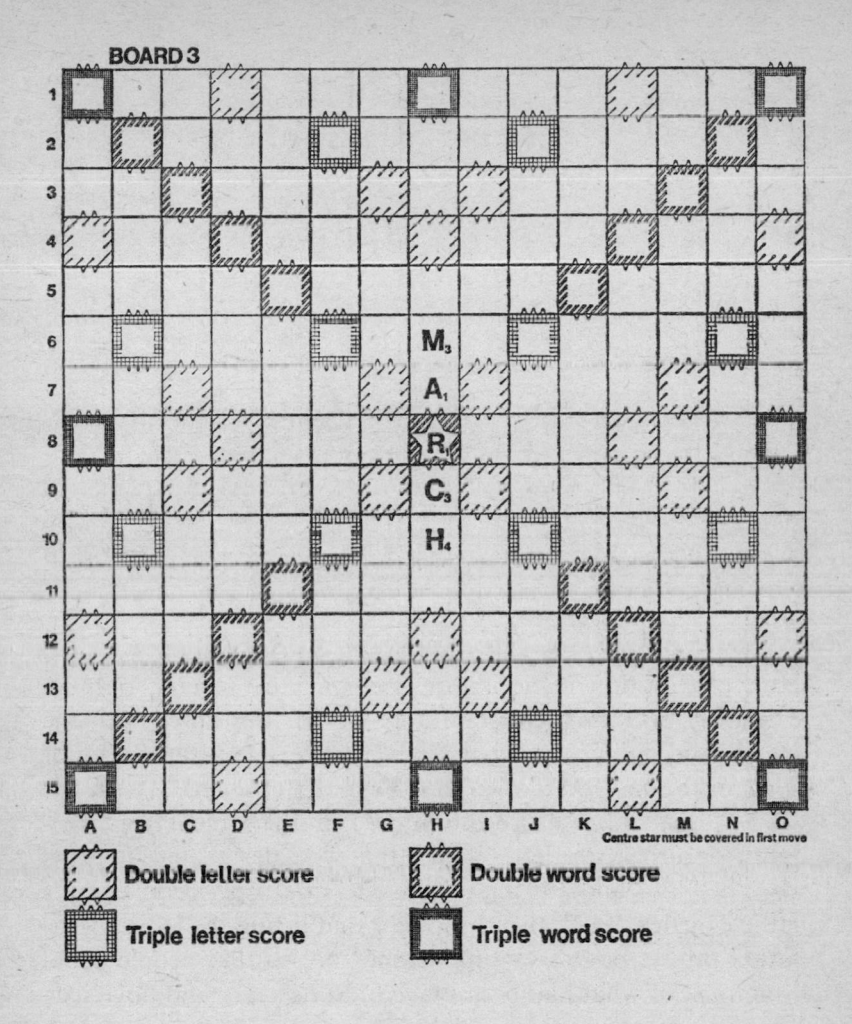

BOARD 3

Centre star must be covered in first move

Double letter score   Double word score

Triple letter score   Triple word score

Letter	Number in set	Value	Letter	Number in set	Value
A	9	1	O	8	1
B	2	3	P	2	3
C	2	3	Q	1	10
D	4	2	R	6	1
E	12	1	S	4	1
F	2	4	T	6	1
G	3	2	U	4	1
H	2	4	V	2	4
I	9	1	W	2	4
J	1	8	X	1	8
K	1	5	Y	2	4
L	4	1	Z	1	10
M	2	3	blank	2	0
N	6	1			

It will help your game if you know something about how the letter distribution came about and why the inventor, Butts, arbitrarily decided there should be 12 tiles imprinted with the letter *E* and only four, say, with the letter *S*. Butts takes a lot of pride in the fact that when Jim Brunot started to market his game 15 years after its invention, he kept the same letter distribution and the same letter values that were designated by Butts when he was hand-pasting paper letters onto plywood squares in the Thirties. 'Back then I thought that listing the letter distribution on the board was important, too, so that people could keep track of what had been played,' Butts said, 'and obviously Jim Brunot thought so, too.'

Several things influenced Butts in the way he portioned out the 100 tiles and the values he gave each letter. 'I had played a lot of anagrams, and I was keen on crosswords, and around that time there was also the fad of cryptograms, and I was interested in them too. I knew that the letter *E* was the most commonly used letter in the alphabet; so it had to be in there more than others. I also went for a lot of *I* tiles because of the opportunities for good endings with *ing* and *ion*. I had trouble with the letter *S* because I wanted to have a fair number of them, but I didn't want to make it too easy for people just to pluralize every word by adding an *S* to words on the board. I decided on four, which is abnormally low, but the two blanks sort of compensated for that because they can be used for *S* too.'

Butts also penalized the *S* by giving it a low face value.

Apart from the face value points that you automatically pick up when you play a tile, you can also reap huge benefits by exploiting the 'premium squares' marked on the board, as shown on Board 4. There are squares which, if you land on them, triple your score for the entire word or words you have just played. Other premium squares can double the value of the word or double or even triple a single letter in the last-played word. The importance of these premium squares is obvious: without them the value of the entire 100 tiles would only add up to 185.

People score in the hundreds (up to 300 in a single turn) by strategically placing their tiles on the triple-word score squares (there are eight of them), on the double-word score squares (there are 16 of them) or on the pink centre square marked by a star, which, besides being the starting point for the game, also means a double-word tally for the lucky starter. Scores are also boosted by landing on a triple-letter square, which means you multiply by three the face value of the specific letter that covers the square. There are 12 triple-letter squares and 24 double-letter squares, for which you multiply by two the face value of the landing tile.

If, in a single turn, you land on a double-letter square with one letter and another lands on a double-word square, the double-letter square is counted first and then the double-word tally is made. This sequence is important.

The triple-word squares, which are placed in each corner of the board and on the edges of an imaginary four-pointed cross, are easy to spot – they are bright red. The double-word squares are pink (like the centre star), the triple-letter squares are dark blue, and the double-letter squares are pale blue.

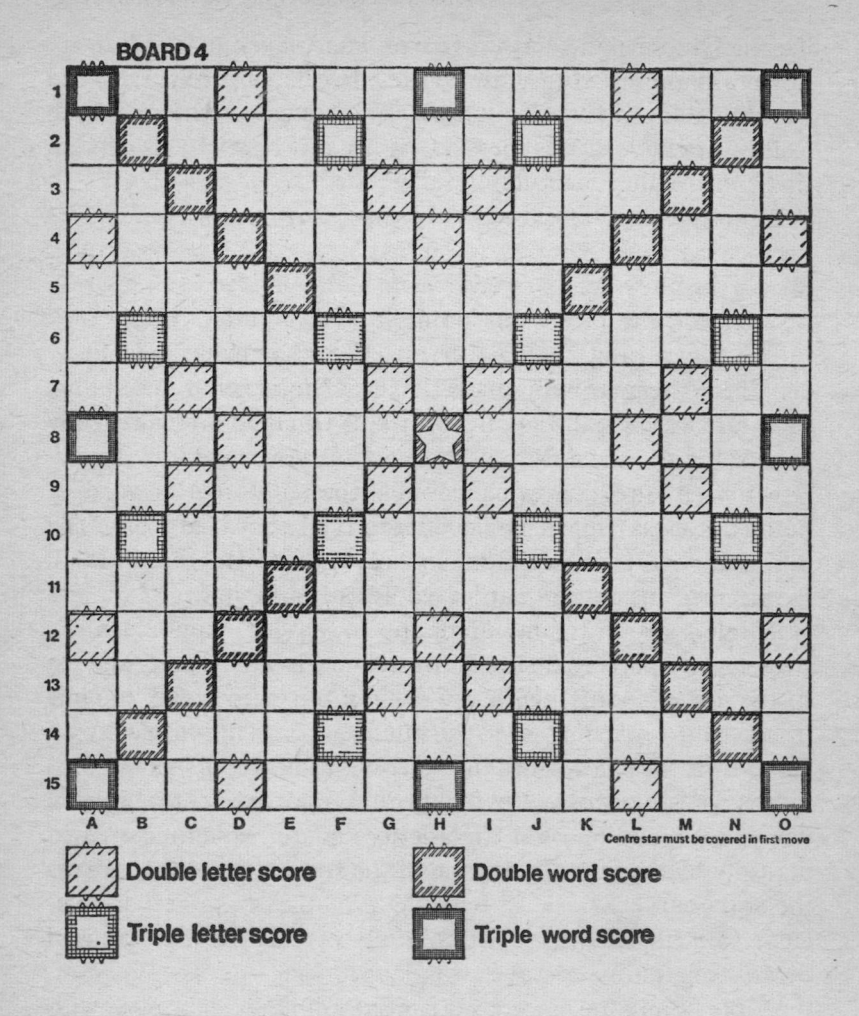

BOARD 4

Centre star must be covered in first move

Double letter score

Double word score

Triple letter score

Triple word score

To reach these high-scoring squares, each player, in turn, can lay down any number of the seven tiles that he has in his rack. He can use all seven letters so long as they make a word and so long as any letters or words that they touch and that are already on the board still constitute complete words. Or the player can place only a single letter on the board to change somebody else's previously played word into a different word. (After each turn, the player draws as many tiles as he has just played to replenish his rack and to keep his tile supply at seven at all times.)

The only restrictions when placing tiles on the board are these: (1) The player can only place tiles in one direction in any one turn. He can place tiles horizontally (Board 5) or vertically (Board 6) to make words. He cannot place tiles diagonally (Board 7). (2) At least one letter of the newly played word must attach to at least one letter already on the board; and after the play, all letter combinations, including the new word, the old word, and any other letters involved, must spell out legitimate words.

The game looks like a crossword puzzle as the interlocking words are formed. Only in this version the clues are all in your head and in your rack. What words you form are completely up to you except for such things as proper nouns, abbreviations, most foreign words, and words with hyphens and apostrophes. These categories of banned words are spelled out in the standard Scrabble rules in the lid of your Scrabble set and are discussed in the next chapter.

To start the game, each player draws one tile. The original Scrabble rules direct players to place all 100 tiles face down on the table before the game and to draw from there whenever tiles are required. A popular alternative, played in Tournament Scrabble and at my Scrabble table, is to use a cloth bag to hold the tiles. After each player has drawn a single letter, he turns it face up, and the one who has drawn the tile nearest the start of the alphabet starts the game. If in a two-man game both players draw the same letter, then they must redraw. If more than two players are involved, then only the ones who have tied in the draw must pick again, and the final jockeying to see who starts

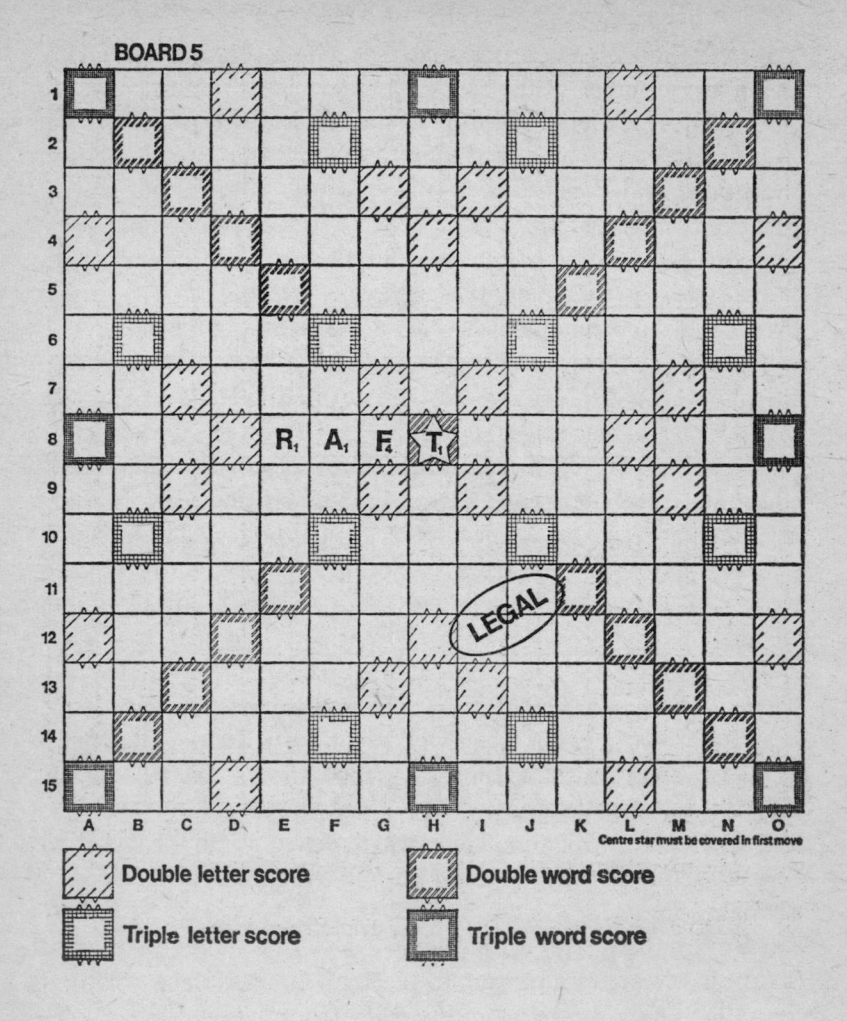

BOARD 5

Double letter score

Double word score

Triple letter score

Triple word score

Centre star must be covered in first move

BOARD 6

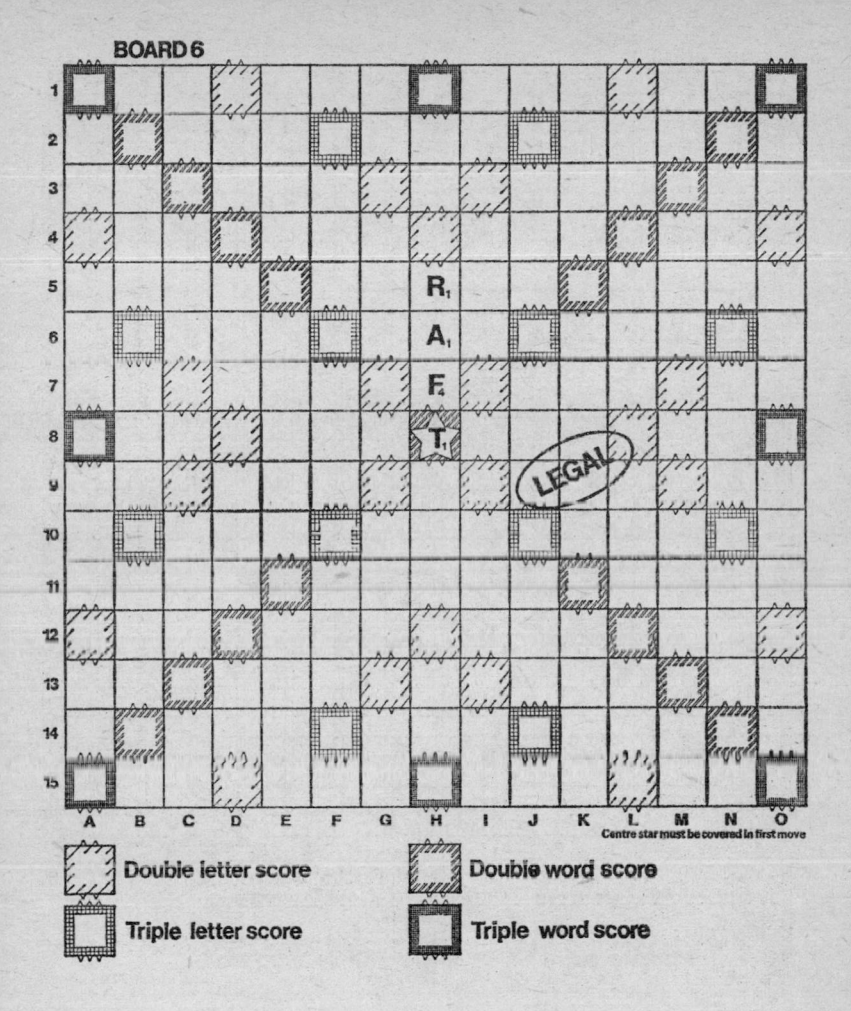

Centre star must be covered in first move

Double letter score

Double word score

Triple letter score

Triple word score

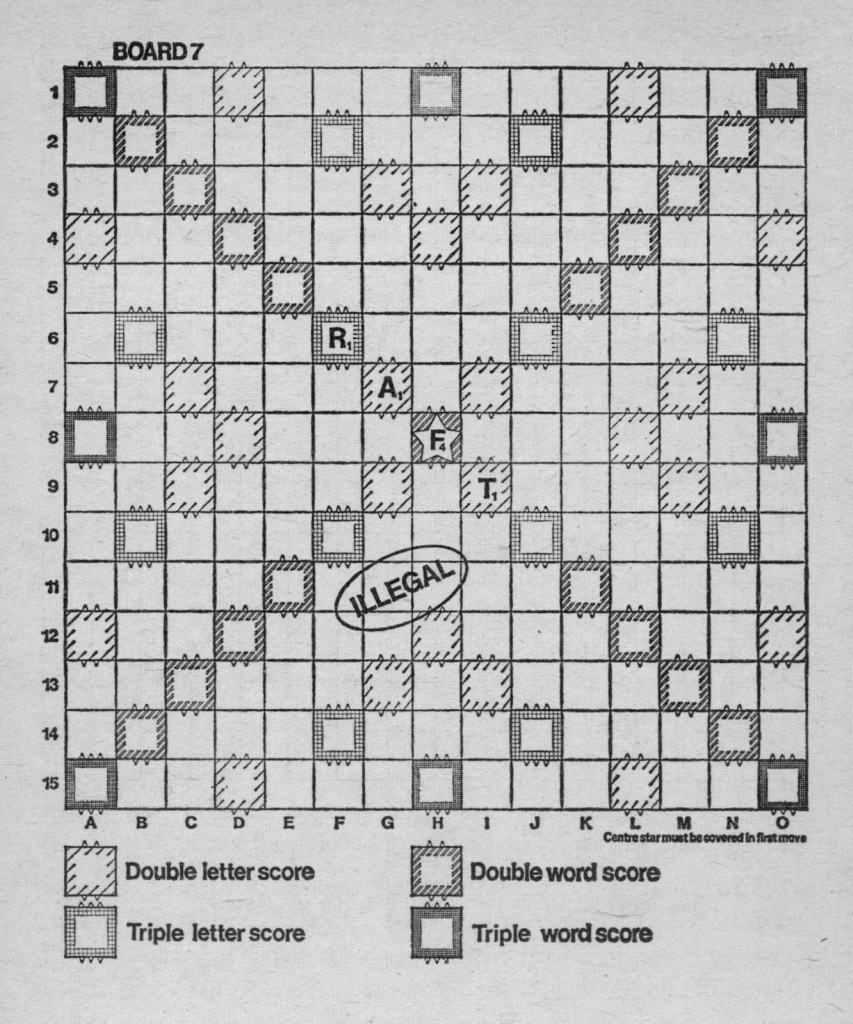

BOARD 7

Double letter score Double word score

Triple letter score Triple word score

first is only between those players. If a player draws the blank, then, since it can be any letter, it is considered the best letter in the alphabet, and he starts. These tiles drawn to determine the 'pole position' are then put back in the pool – on the table or in the bag – and reshuffled. All players then draw seven fresh tiles, sight unseen.

There are different rules for starts (see the chapter on game variations), but the standard beginning is for the starter to place any word on the board as long as it consists of two or more letters and as long as one of those letters covers the star in the middle of the board.

In the sample game on Board 8, the first player places the word *raft* on the board, making sure that one letter covers the centre star. He could play the word horizontally, but, quite legally, runs it down the middle of the board.

For that move the player gets the total of all the face values of his four played tiles, which add up to 7 points. None of his tiles land on premium word squares, but because he has started and because one tile, in this case the letter *T*, covers the centre star, his word score is automatically doubled, and he scores a total of 14 points for the move.

His score is recorded on a scorepad, but before this is done, the opposing player (or players if you are playing a three- or four-man game) has the right to challenge the fact that *raft* is indeed a word. If the challenged word does not appear in whatever dictionary is being used as the 'house Bible', then the player must pick up his tiles, his score is disallowed, and he forfeits his turn. In basic Scrabble there is no penalty for the challenger if somebody challenges a word and the word is found to be legitimate; the same is true of the British National Championships, which follow the standard rules. However, in American and Australian tournament play and many house rules, the challenger who loses a dispute must then forfeit his own next turn. This makes challenging an important part of Scrabble strategy, and how, when, and why you challenge are detailed in the strategy section of this book.

Once a word is down and the score has been tallied and

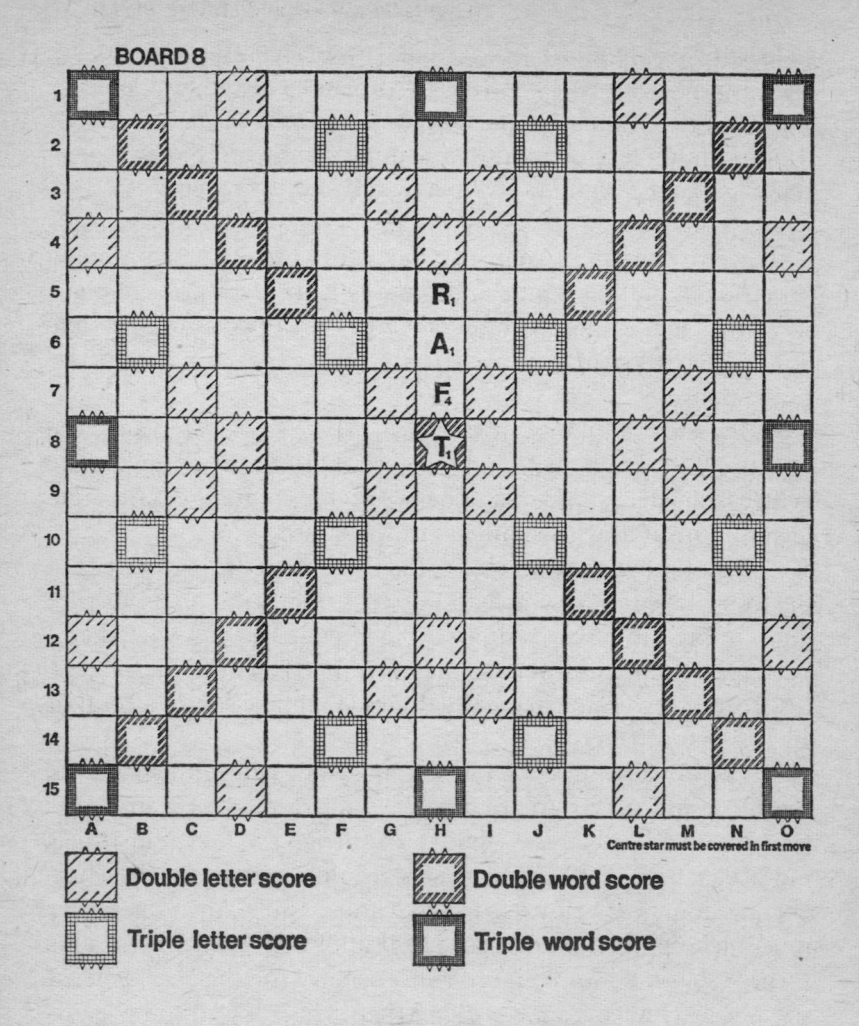

BOARD 8

Centre star must be covered in first move

Double letter score   Double word score

Triple letter score   Triple word score

recorded, it cannot be moved from that position or removed from the board, even if for some reason it is later discovered that the word does not really exist.

The first player then draws four fresh tiles, again sight unseen, to bring his rack back up to the standard seven tiles. The second player then moves. He has the following options: If he has the necessary tiles, he can extend the word *raft* at either end or at both ends to create words like *craft*, *crafty*, *rafts* or *rafter*. Or using tiles in his rack and letters already on the board, he can build a totally new word as long as one of his letters hooks on to some part of the existing word.

Player 2 plays the horizontal word *strand* on Board 9, using the letters *S*, *R*, *A*, *N* and *D* from his own hand and utilizing the *T* placed on the board previously by his opponent. For that he scores 9 points. He gets 4 points for the letter *D* because it lands on a double-letter square and the *D* has a face value of 2 points, and he gets 1 point each for the *s-t-r-a-n*. You will notice that he still gets the credit for the face value of the *T* even though the letter was put there by his opponent. If, however, the *T* had been originally placed on a double-word square or a double-letter square, those premiums would not have been assessed again.

Once a premium square has been covered, and this applies to double- and triple-word squares as well, it is dead. Only the face values of tiles are counted in any later action.

Whether or not Player 2 should have played that word at all is a different story, and that is discussed in detail in the strategy part of the book. What we are interested in here is getting a game going.

For example, though, if, instead of playing the word *strand*, the player had added the word *sand* in Board 10 to the top of the existing word, he would have scored far better. He would have turned the word *raft* into the word *draft* and would have counted the *D* as a double-letter score going each way. He would have also received full marks, at face value, of the *r-a-f-t* vertically plus the double-letter tally for the *D* as well as the total for the word *sand* horizontally. This is a major scoring point in Scrabble. Any time you alter an existing word on the board, you receive

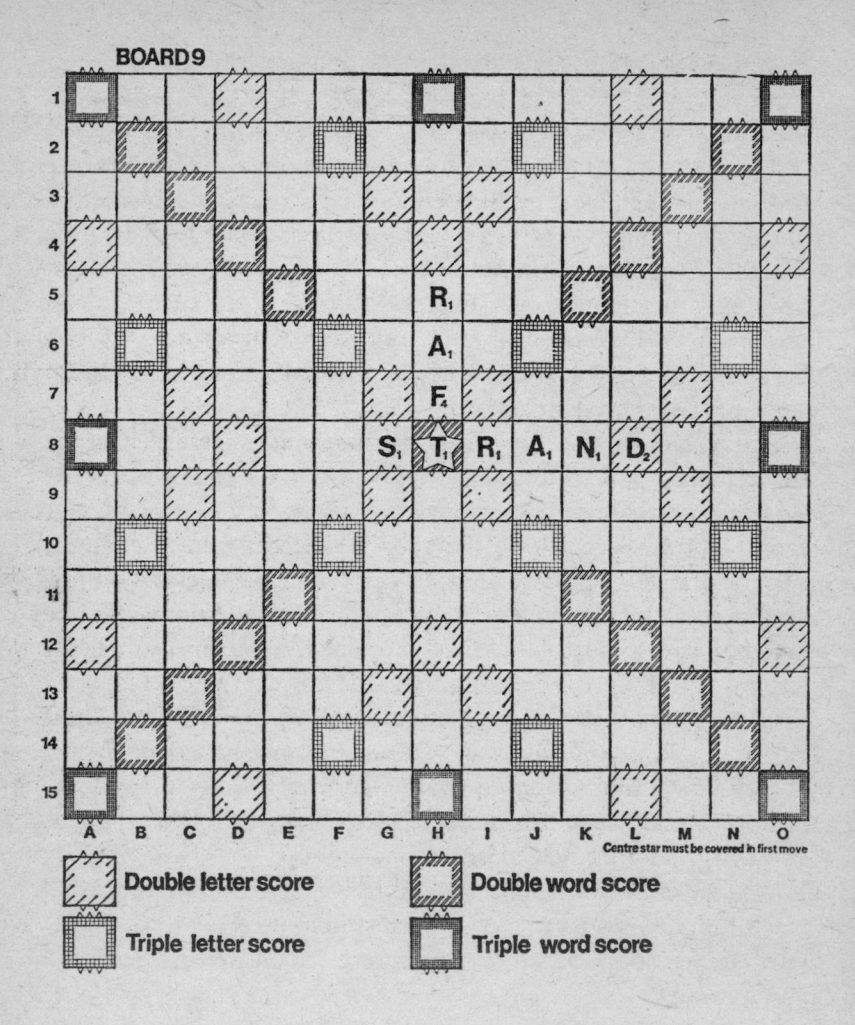

BOARD 9

Centre star must be covered in first move

Double letter score Double word score

Triple letter score Triple word score

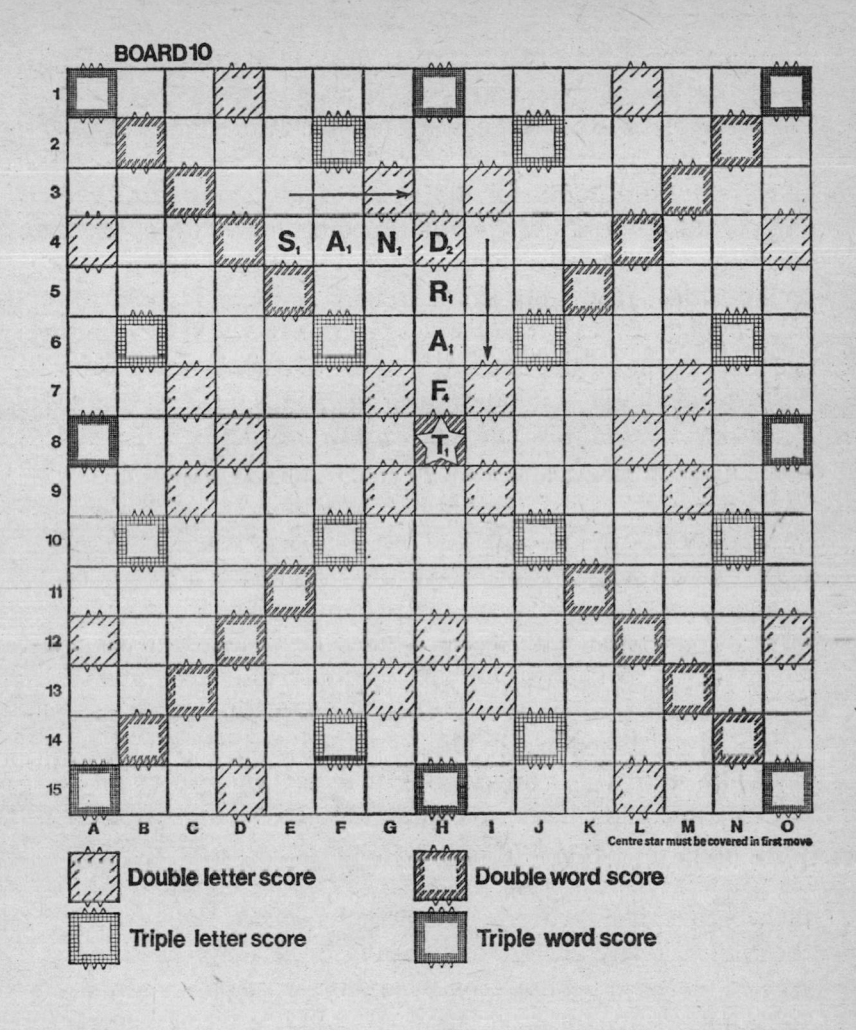

BOARD 10

Double letter score   Double word score

Triple letter score   Triple word score

credit for the new word's complete face value – no matter how much of it was placed there previously by an opponent.

Playing the word *sand* and turning *raft* into *draft* would have given Player 2 a score of 18. You will notice the player would have received 4 points for the *D* in his word *sand* (2×2) and then would have received another 4 points for the *D* in the vertical word *draft* because both ways the letter hit a double-letter square. Indicatively, his score would have been 11 points for amending the existing word and 7 for his new word. So you can see that exploiting an opponent's word is a basic Scrabble tactic. The reason Player 2 did not receive any points from the original word *raft* was that his ultimate word *strand* did not change the original word at all even though it was attached to both sides of it.

Anyway let's ignore what the second player could have done and concentrate on what he did do. The board now has *raft* going vertically and the word *strand* intersecting it.

The first player, with his rack restocked, now does what is called tightening the board. By using just a few letters, he weaves his new word through letters already on the board and scores points in all directions. In Board 11 he plays the word *most* vertically so that it involves both of the existing words on the board and creates three new ones. He gets 7 points from the word *most*, including 3 for the *M*, 2 for the *O* because it hits a double-letter square, 1 for the *S* already on the board, and 2 for the *T* because it also covers a double-letter square. But by placing those tiles snugly against the existing ones, Player 1 has also created the word *ma* horizontally and the word *of* horizontally; so he must get credit for those words, too. He gets 4 points for *ma* (a vulgar but legitimate word) which means his three-point *M* has actually been worth 6 points, and he gets 6 points for the word *of*.

His total for the turn is *most*, 8 points; *ma*, 4; *of*, 6; total, 18 points. This is added to his first turn score of 14 to give him a cumulative score of 32.

Player 2, now trailing, has luckily drawn the *Z*, one of the four big guns, while restocking his hand. The other three most valued

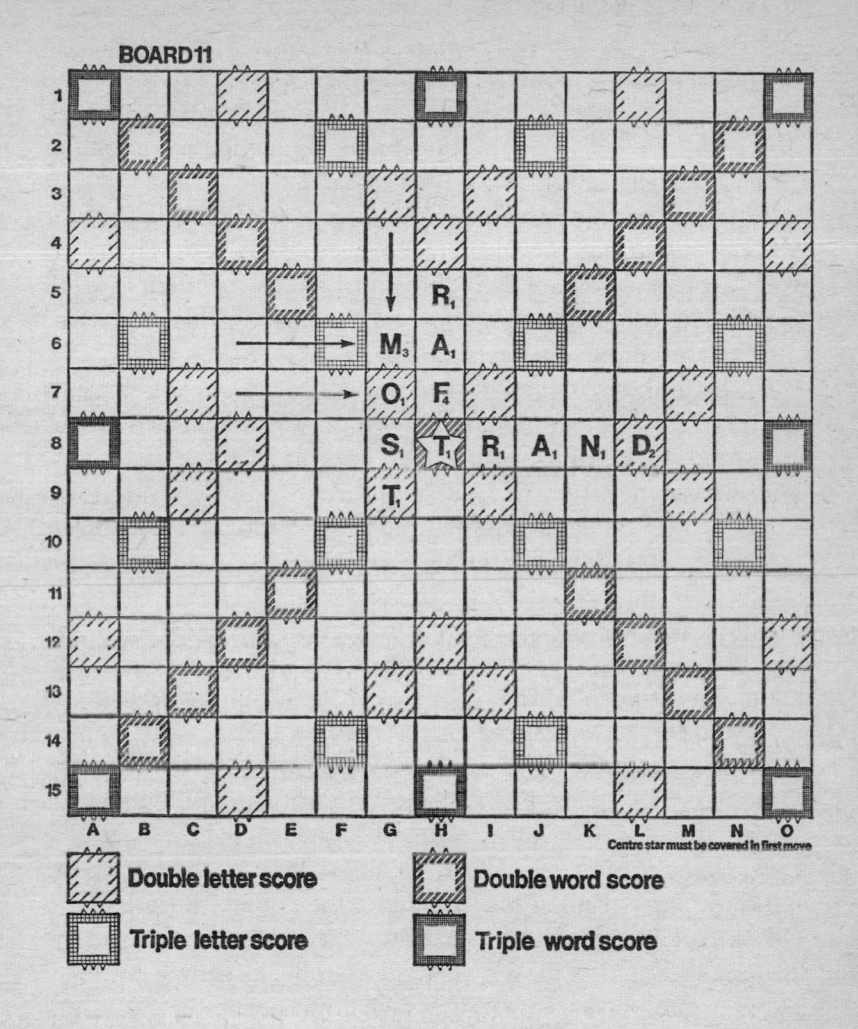

BOARD 11

Centre star must be covered in first move

⬚ Double letter score		⬚ Double word score
☐ Triple letter score		☐ Triple word score

letters are the *Q*, *X* and *J*. Although he missed the word *draft*, he pounces on the same opportunity this turn in Board 12 and turns *raft* into *craft* while making the word *crazy* across the top. He doesn't have a letter *Y* in his hand, by he does have one of the blanks so he calls that a *Y*.

When a blank lands on a double-letter score, it is meaningless. A blank is worth zero, and zero doubled is still zero. However, when a blank lands on a double-word square or a triple-word square, it most definitely counts – as it does in this case. This move is a good one, and gets Player 2 a total of 49 points.

The breakdown is like this. For the word *crazy*, he gets 6 points for the *C* (it lands on a double-letter square), 1 point each for the *R* and the *A*, 10 points for the *Z* and nothing for the blank substituting for the letter *Y*. That is a total of 18, which is doubled because the blank is on a pink double-word square. He also gets another 6 points for the *C* going vertically in the word *craft* plus 7 points for the face value of *raft*. A total of 49.

Unless you are playing a variation of the game called Blank (or Ecology) Scrabble, in which the blank can be used again and again, then the substitute *Y* remains there for the rest of the game and for the remainder must remain as a *Y*.

Player 2 now adds his 49 points to his opening 9 to take the lead with 58 for two turns. Player 1, possibly caught with bad letters and an abundance of low-scoring tiles, such as two or three *O*'s, tries to get rid of them. He can, at any time, use a turn to 'pass' and return any or all of his letters into the pool for a fresh draw. This is explained in detail – the how, when and why of it – in the strategy section. If a player wishes to redraw, he forfeits his turn, places the no longer wanted tiles face down next to his rack, and draws a corresponding number of fresh tiles. The unwanted tiles are then placed back in the pool and the other player takes another turn. Instead of passing, though, Player 1 decides to 'dump' some of his offending tiles – he accepts a low score to get rid of tiles of which he has more than one of a kind in his hand. On Board 13 he plays the word *tool*, tucking it up under the previously played *strand*.

For that he gets 5 points for *tool* (the *L* is doubled because it

BOARD 12

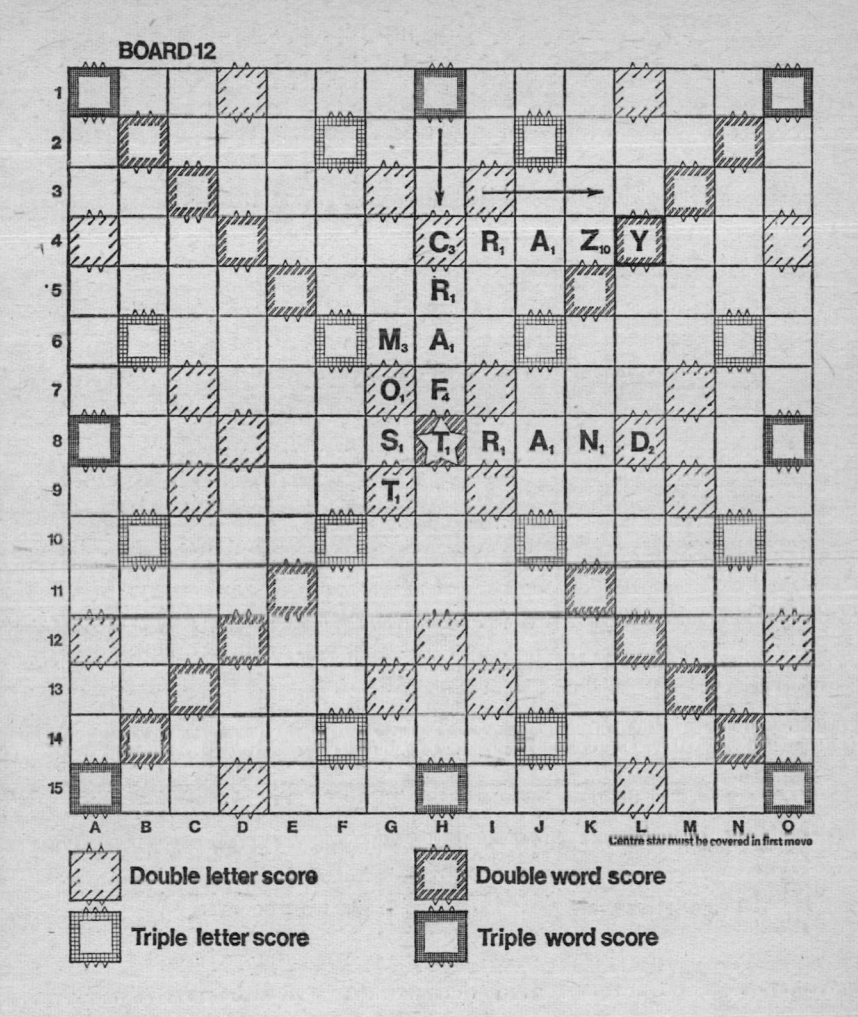

Double letter score   Double word score

Triple letter score   Triple word score

Centre star must be covered in first move

BOARD 13

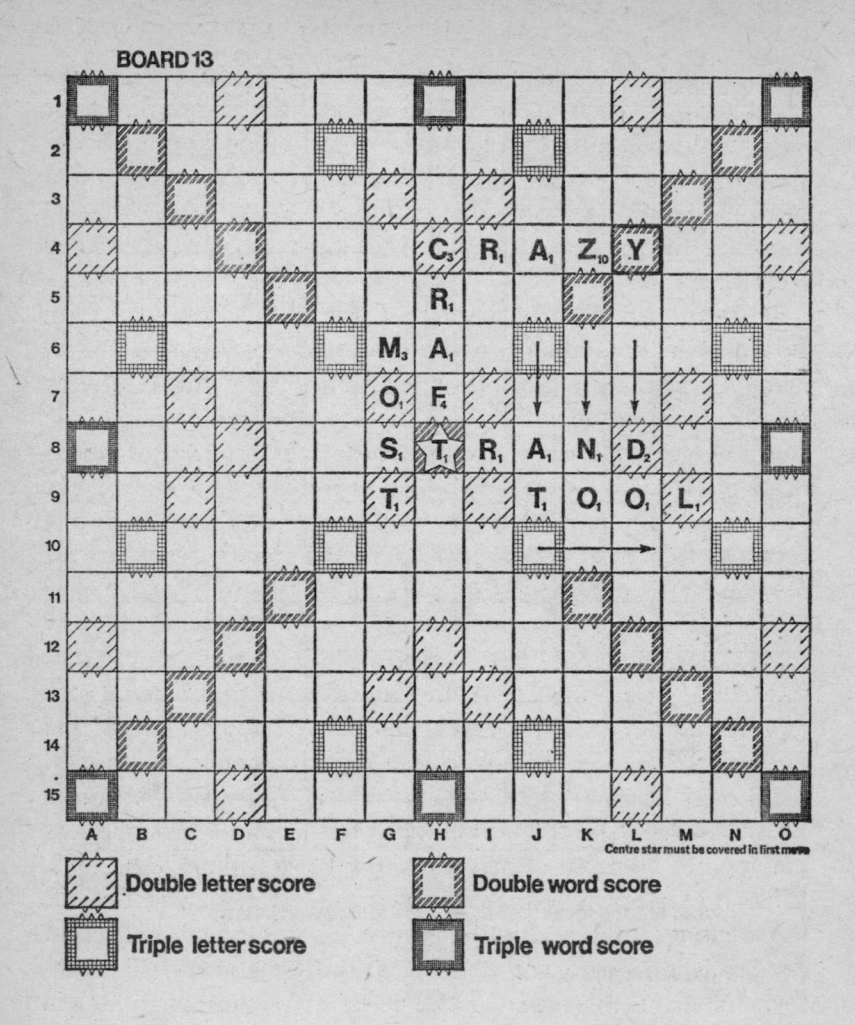

Double letter score   Double word score

Triple letter score   Triple word score

Centre star must be covered in first move

hits a double-letter square), and he gets points for making the short vertical words *at*, *no* and *do*. He gets 2 points for *at*, 2 for *no*, and although the *D* of his third word *do* is on a double-letter square, it is only scored at face value because it was played in a previous turn and the double count was used then. The total score for his four words is only 12, but he can now draw four fresh tiles.

His opponent has the letters *E E C I L N S* in his hand. On Board 14 he unjumbles them to make the word *license* and re-arranges them again to get the word *silence*. He finally returns to *license*, running the word down the board and pluralizing *tool*. For that he gets 17 points for the word *license* (the *C* and final *E* hit triple-letter squares), and he gets 5 points for the word *tools*. He also gets a bonus of 50 points because he used all seven letters in his hand in one play. So his total score for the turn is 17 for *license*, 50 for the bonus, and 5 for *tools* for a total of 72. If he had played the word *silence* (Board 15), he would have got slightly more because it would have run down into a double-word score for a total of 22 plus 50 for the bonus word plus 5 points for *tools* for a total of 77. However, that would have left an enticing opening for a good triple-word score for his opponent, as indicated by the arrows on Board 15. With the *E* in such a position, he would also have laid himself open to the risk of his opponent playing out all seven of his letters to hit *two* triple word scores. When that happens, a score is tripled and retripled, which means the original total is multiplied by nine. That is the one move that can produce a score of more than 200 and sometimes even higher than 300 in a single turn. Careful defensive positioning of letters – as described here – will be discussed in greater detail in the strategy section.

And so the game goes on with each player filling in the cross-word, building off his own previous turns and his opponent's, and replenishing his rack from the pool until the supply of tiles is depleted.

The game can end in either of two ways: (1) With no tiles left in the pool, one player uses up all the remaining tiles in his rack and goes out; play immediately stops, or (2) Both players still

BOARD 14

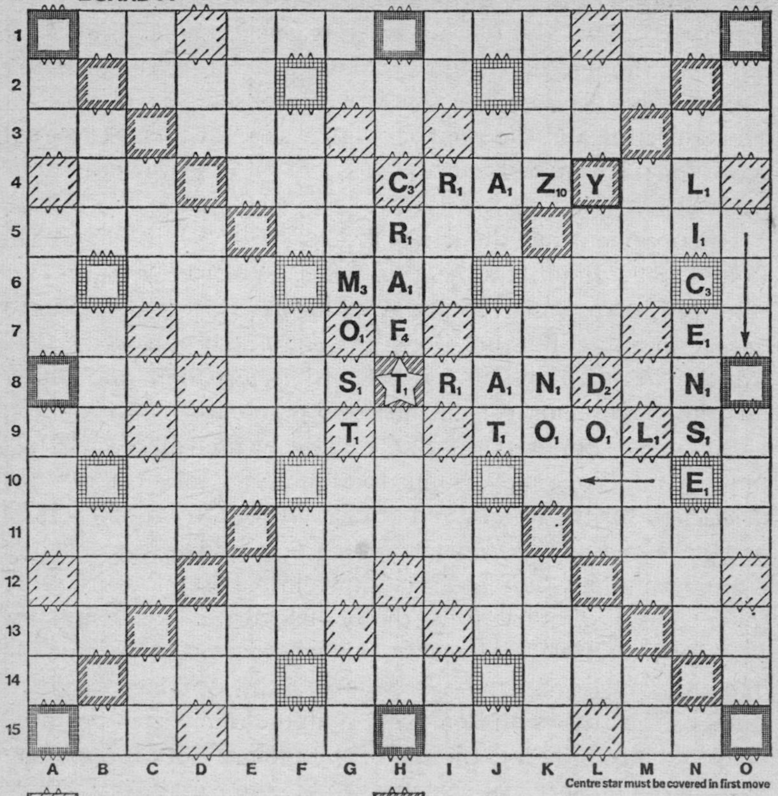
Centre star must be covered in first move

Double letter score

Double word score

Triple letter score

Triple word score

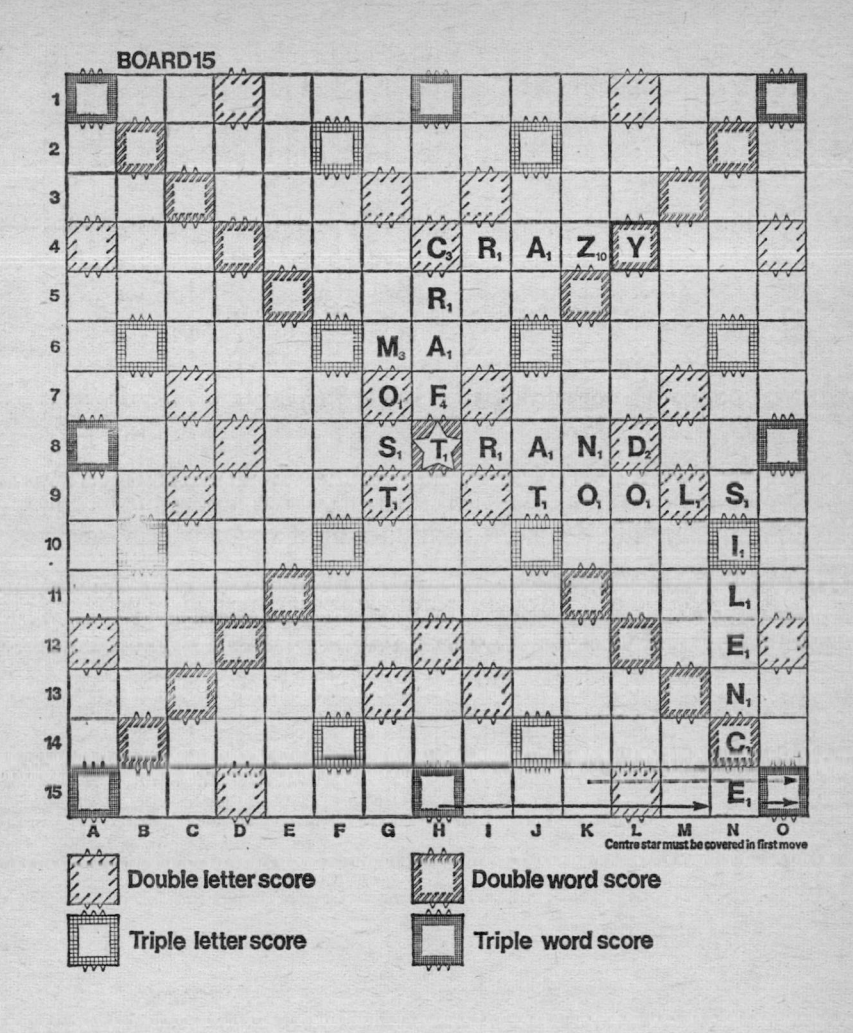

BOARD 15

Centre star must be covered in first move

Double letter score

Double word score

Triple letter score

Triple word score

have tiles in their racks but cannot find any place on the board where the remaining letters can be placed to make words. This often happens when players are caught with tricky consonants near the end and especially if one is caught with the *Q* and has no *U* to go with it.

If the first ending occurs, the players with tiles remaining have the face values of these tiles deducted from their total scores. The player who went out has his score increased by the value of opponents' tiles still unplayed. A common variation of this is for the player who goes out to receive double the face value of the opponent's remaining tiles while the other player deducts nothing from his own hand. Once a player goes out, all play stops even if an opponent has an opening for his remaining tiles. Some people do play under a house rule that going out first is unimportant and the game continues until anybody and everybody who can make a move has done so.

If the second ending occurs and no player can shed all his tiles, then each player deducts his own remaining tiles from his total.

The person with the highest total at the end, after all the accounting has been done, is the winner, even if another player was the one who went out first.

2 Basic Scrabble Rules

To Start

All 100 tiles should be turned face down on the table and thoroughly shuffled. Unplayed tiles remain face down on the table as a 'tile pool' throughout the game. As mentioned earlier, a popular alternative is to place all the tiles in a deep cloth bag and to use that as a receptacle. It is imperative, whichever method is used, to make sure the tile faces remain hidden until drawn from the pool and played on the board.

Each player draws one tile to determine who gets the privilege of starting the game. The player drawing the letter nearest the beginning of the alphabet starts the game. If two players draw the same low letter, they must redraw. If a player draws a blank, it is considered the best tile, since it may be any letter; in some house rules the player drawing a blank starts even if another player draws an *A*.

The 'starting position' tiles are then all returned to the tile bag or tile heap and reshuffled. One variation of this is for each player to have the choice of rejecting the first tile or keeping it. Starting with the lead-off player and rotating to the left, each player now draws seven new tiles (or six if you are playing the start variation) and the tiles are placed on the racks in front of each player.

The Play

1 The Opening: Using two or more of his letters, the first player forms a word and places it on the board either horizontally or vertically. Horizontal words must read from left to right, and vertical words must read from top to bottom. Diagonal words are not permitted. The only restriction on the starting player's positioning for his word is that one letter, any letter, must cover the centre star square. Some house rules set minimums for the length of the starting word, ranging from four letters up to seven letters, and this variation, called 'Jacks to Open' or 'Aces to Open', is explained in the variations chapter.

As a starting bonus for covering the centre star, the first player doubles his total score for the word. If he wishes, however, or if he does not have a word to play, he may forfeit his turn and Player 2 gets the chance to start the game. Under that circumstance, the second player would get the starting bonus. The first player who passes may use that turn to exchange any, or all, of the tiles in his rack.

2 Completing a Turn: A player finishes his turn by adding up his score for that move and announcing it before entering it on a score sheet. He then draws as many new tiles as he has played to bring his rack back up to the original seven tiles. This restocking procedure must be done immediately after each turn and should become automatic.

3 Successive Moves: Play passes to the left. Player 2 – and then each successive player – adds one or more letters to those already on the board to form a new word or new words, as on Board 16. All letters played in any single turn must be placed in one row across or down the board. At least one new letter must touch a letter already on the board. Letters can be placed at either end of existing words or in the middle, if space is available, or as links to join several letter groupings into one word as on Board 17. On Board 16 a player has used the letter *H* from the word *arch* to make the vertical word *heal*; the letter *L* from *heal* has been utilized in a following turn to make the horizontal word *lend*, and the *D* from *lend* has then been used in constructing the vertical word *good*. Then, on Board 17, a player has legally used an *M* at the start of the word *arch* plus the letters *I, N* in the middle to tie up with an existing *G* to make the word *marching*. The same thing applies on Board 18, where in two turns *heal* becomes *health* and *lend* becomes *blending*.

BOARD 16

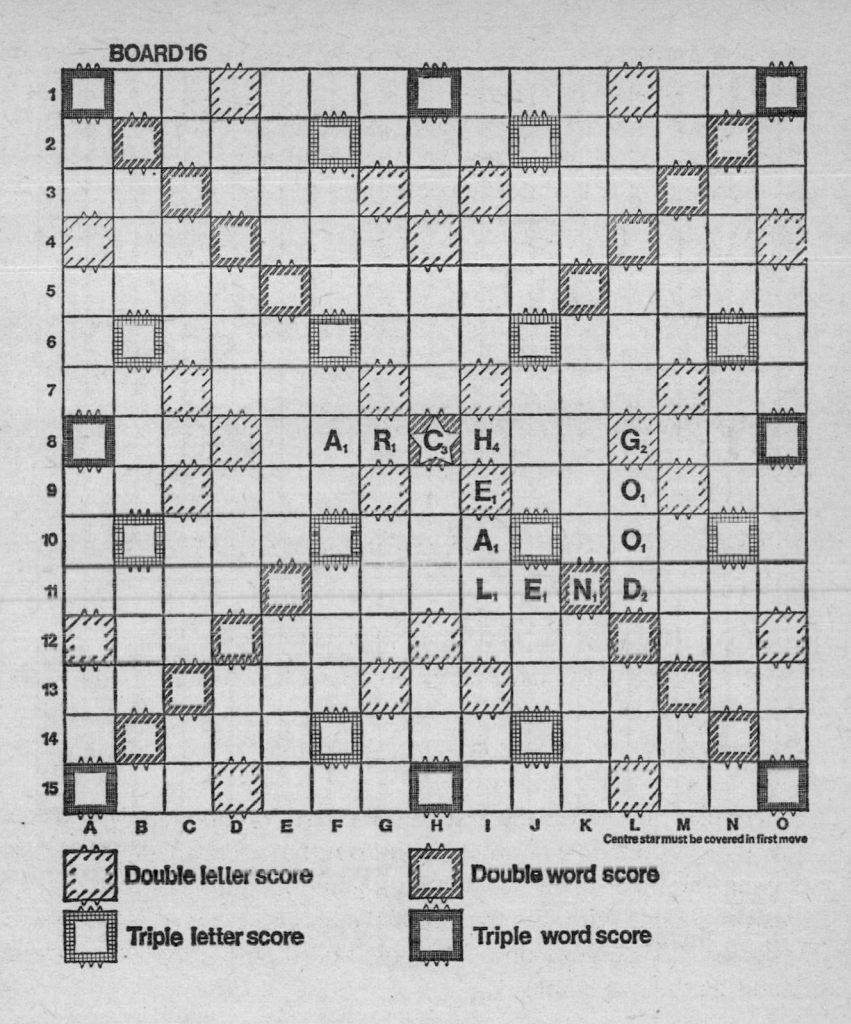

Centre star must be covered in first move

Double letter score

Double word score

Triple letter score

Triple word score

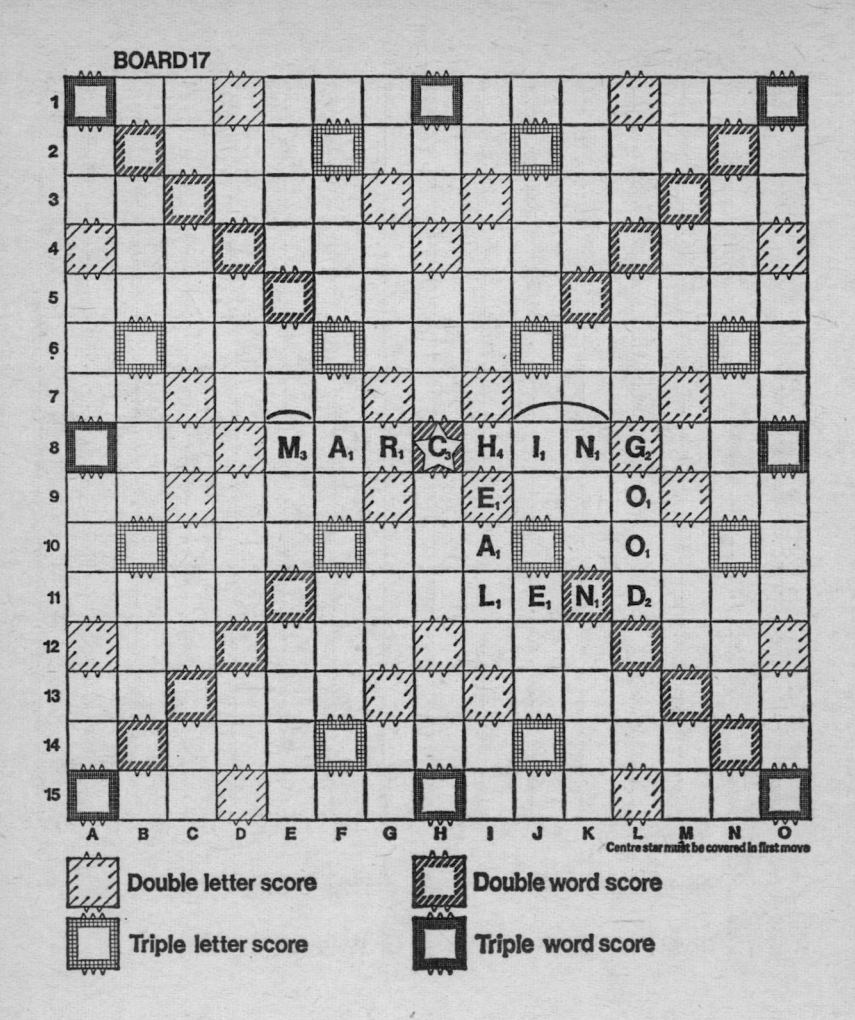

BOARD 17

Centre star must be covered in first move

Double letter score Double word score

Triple letter score Triple word score

BOARD 18

Double letter score

Triple letter score

Double word score

Triple word score

Centre star must be covered in first move

Any time letters are placed on the board, they must form a complete word or words; and if at the same time they touch other letters in adjacent rows, they must also, crossword fashion, form complete words with those letters, no matter if they are horizontal or vertical. As long as that stipulation is honoured, players can place parallel words like the example on Board 19.

4 Letter Placement: Once a letter has been played, it may not be shifted. The only exception is when you are playing such variations as Anagram Scrabble or Blank (or Ecology) Scrabble, and even then the exception must be spelled out before the start of the game.

5 Blank Tiles: The two blank tiles are 'wild cards', which may be used as any letter. When playing a blank, the player must announce what letter it represents. It cannot be shifted or have its designation changed for the remainder of the game. The exception is when you are playing Blank (or Ecology) Scrabble, in which blanks may be recycled again and again.

6 Passing: Any player may use his turn, as mentioned in Rule 1, to replace any or all of the letters in his rack. He does this by discarding the unwanted letters face down alongside his rack. He draws the same number of new letters from the tile bag or tile pool, checks to make sure he has drawn the correct number, then discards the old letters back into the pool and shuffles. He may not touch the board or play a word as part of a passing turn. Passing may be done, in turn, at any time, according to the standard British rules. However, American and Australian rules ban tile-changing once there are only seven letters or less in the pool. After that point is reached, passing, without an exchange of tiles, is permitted, but all letter-changing is banned. After passing, a player awaits his next turn.

An unusual passing variation, played under some house rules, permits a player to throw back tiles without penalty after restocking his rack if he has three or more of the same letters in his hand. Under this variation, he may throw back all duplicates, in excess of two, without penalty and draw fresh tiles.

If any player passes for three consecutive turns, he forfeits the

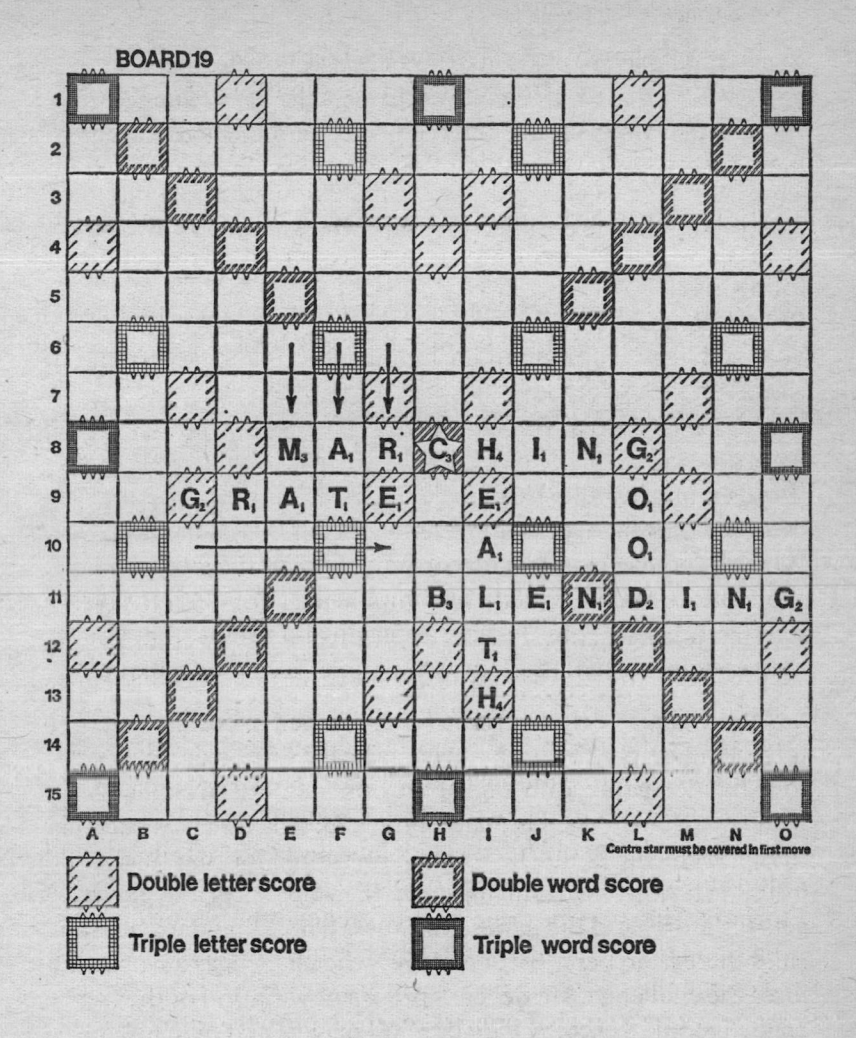

BOARD 19

Centre star must be covered in first move

- ▨ Double letter score
- ▨ Double word score
- ▨ Triple letter score
- ▨ Triple word score

game. If all players pass three times consecutively, then the game is terminated. Each player deducts the face values of his seven tiles from his total, and the player with the highest score remaining wins the game.

7 Words: Any words found in a standard dictionary (you should agree on which one before you start) are permitted except the following:

Proper names

Words that are capitalized, including months and days of the week

Words designated as foreign words

Abbreviations

Words requiring apostrophes

Words requiring hyphens.

Words that take normal declensions, comparatives and superlatives are permitted even if not in a dictionary if the book of reference spells out the fact, as usually is the case, that you may assume normal transformation unless otherwise stipulated.

8 Challenging: Any word may be challenged once it is on the board and before the next player starts his turn. In a three- or four-handed game, only one of the opponents need challenge. If the word challenged is unacceptable, the player takes back his tiles, forfeits the points he would have scored for that turn, and loses his turn. If the challenge fails, the word stays, the player gets his score, and the game continues. Under standard Scrabble rules there is no penalty for a player who challenges a word and loses the challenge. However, a prevalent variation of the challenge rule – used by a lot of good players and in many tournaments – stipulates that if a challenger fails to uphold his challenge, he forfeits his next turn as a penalty. In a multihanded game all players who joined in the challenge would forfeit their turn. Another, more vicious, variation is for an unsuccessful challenger not only to lose a turn but also to be penalized by the number of points the disputed play is worth.

The dictionary may not be used for browsing and can only be consulted to settle legal challenges. A word must be challenged

before the next player starts his turn. If it escapes detection, a
phoney word remains on the board and is scored normally.
The word can be challenged later if modified by a subsequent
play. In that circumstance, however, the modifier takes full
responsibility for the original root word. A disputed word
cannot be traced back to its source.

9 The End: Play continues until all the tiles have been drawn and
one player has used all of his final seven letters. If no player can
go out, play stops by mutual agreement after each player has
played his rack to a standstill.

Scoring

1 The Scorer: One player is elected scorer and keeps a
cumulative tally of each player's score. Ideally, each player
should keep a pad and pencil in front of him and keep track of
all scores, but most people usually leave the job to the player
who is quickest at arithmetic.

2 The Scoring Procedure: The score for each turn is calculated
by adding up the face values of all the letters in all the words
formed or modified in the play and then adding bonus points
scored by landing tiles on 'premium squares'.

3 Premium Letter Squares: Premium letter squares are shown
heavily outlined on Board 20. A light blue square *doubles* the
score of a letter placed on it; a dark blue square *triples* the score
of a letter placed on it.

4 Premium Word Squares: Premium word squares are shown
heavily outlined on Board 21. The score for the entire *word* is
doubled when one of its letters lands on a pink square. When a
letter lands on a red square, the score for the entire *word* is
tripled. Premiums, if any, for double- or triple-letter squares
should be included in the score before the word total is doubled
or tripled.

5 Double Bonuses: When two or more words are formed in the
same move and when a letter on a premium square features in
both the horizontal and vertical words, then the common letter

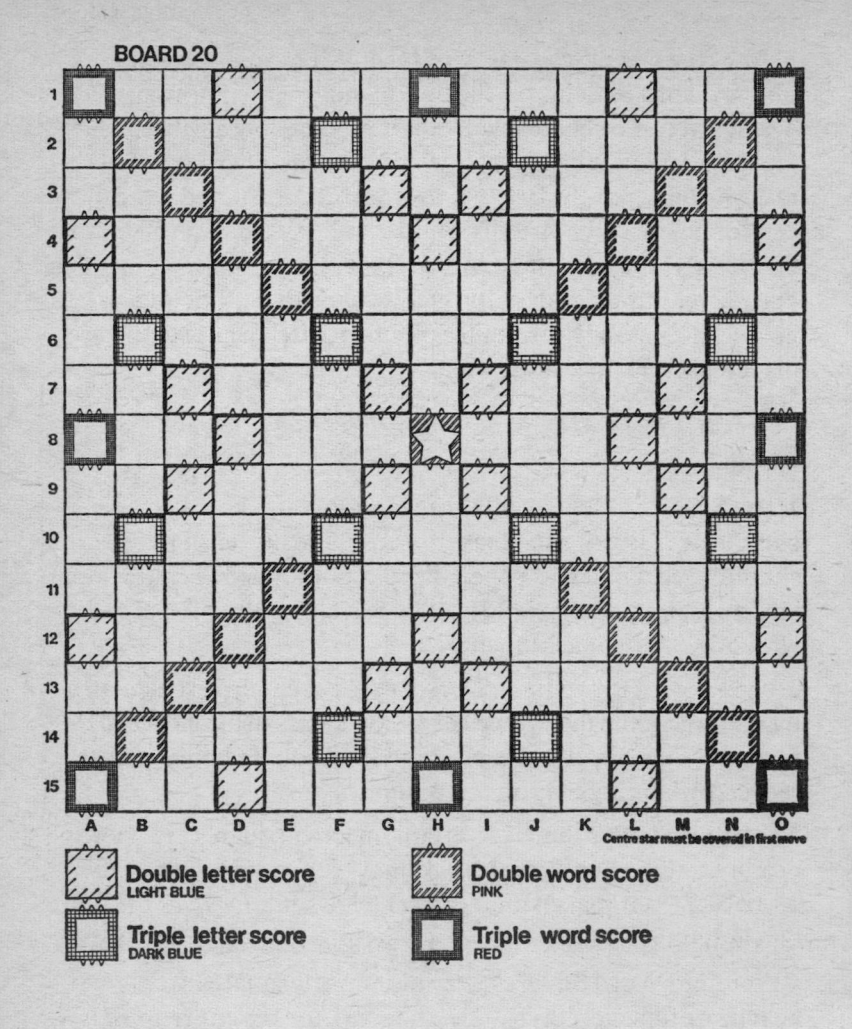

BOARD 20

Centre star must be covered in first move

	Double letter score
	LIGHT BLUE
	Triple letter score
	DARK BLUE

	Double word score
	PINK
	Triple word score
	RED

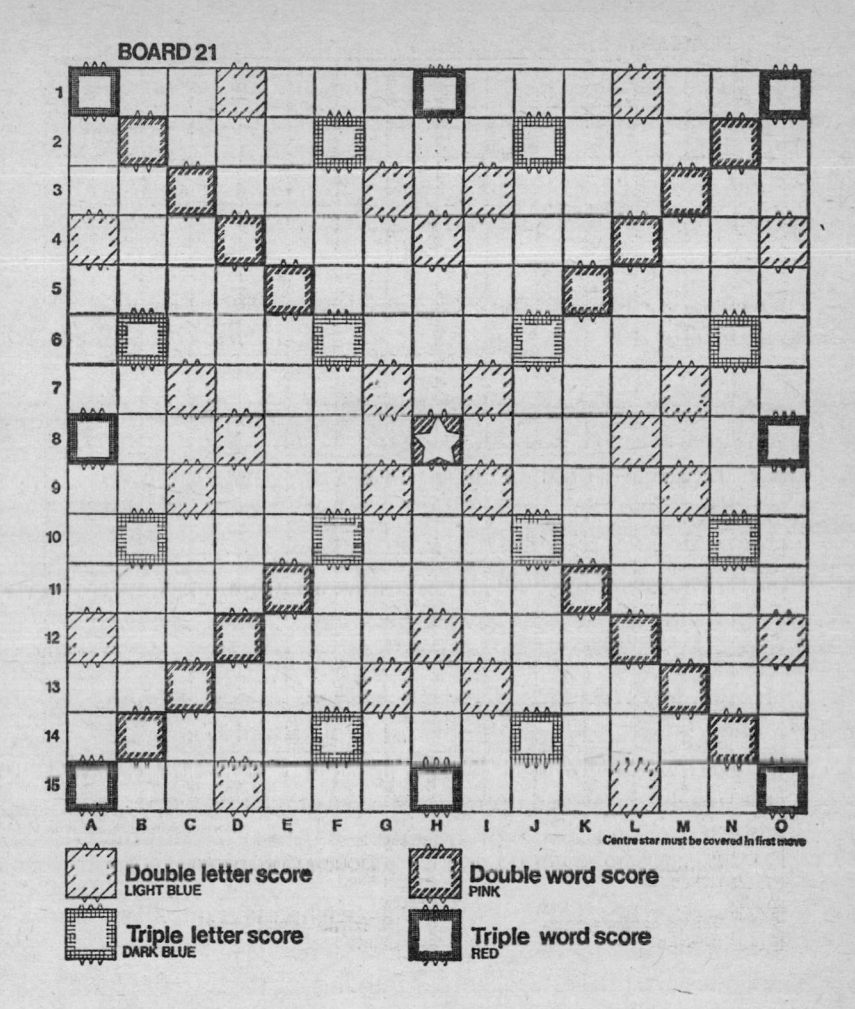

BOARD 21

is counted with full bonus value in each direction (see Board 22). In this case, the letter *K* is worth 15 points for landing on a triple-letter square in the word *think*, which is then doubled because the letter *T* lands on a double-word square. However, the *K* is also worth 15 points for extending *pin* into *pink*, as well as collecting the face value of the letters *P I N*.

6 Other Bonuses: If a word is formed that covers two premium word squares, the score is *doubled* and then *redoubled* (see Board 23) for four times the letter count, or it is *tripled* and then *retripled* for nine times the letter count, as the case may be. Although most of the premium word squares are more than seven squares apart, you can reach more than one in a turn by using tiles already on the board as stepping stones.

As mentioned earlier, the centre star is a pink square and therefore doubles the total of the opening word score.

7 Limits on Premiums: The letter and word premiums apply only in the turn in which they are first played. Once covered, they score at face value only.

8 The Blanks: The blank tiles are basically worth zero points. If a blank tiles lands on a double- or triple-letter square, the value is still zero. Twice nothing is nothing. However, if a blank lands on a double-word premium square or a triple-word premium square, the sum of the letters in the word is doubled or trebled even though the blank is valueless by itself.

9 Seven-letter Bonus Plays: Any player who plays out all seven letters in his rack in a single turn scores a bonus of 50 points. The bonus is added after all other tallying for the turn has been completed. If, for example, a player lays down a bonus word with a tile value of 40 points, which then doubles to 80 because he lands on a double-word square, he then adds the bonus 50 for a total of 130. He does not add the 50-point bonus to the original 40 before doubling for a final score of 180. Any number of seven-letter plays can be scored in a game, and a player gets his 50-point bonus each time. The bonus is for dropping all seven tiles at once, and therefore you can get only one bonus per turn – no matter how many words are formed by your seven-letter play.

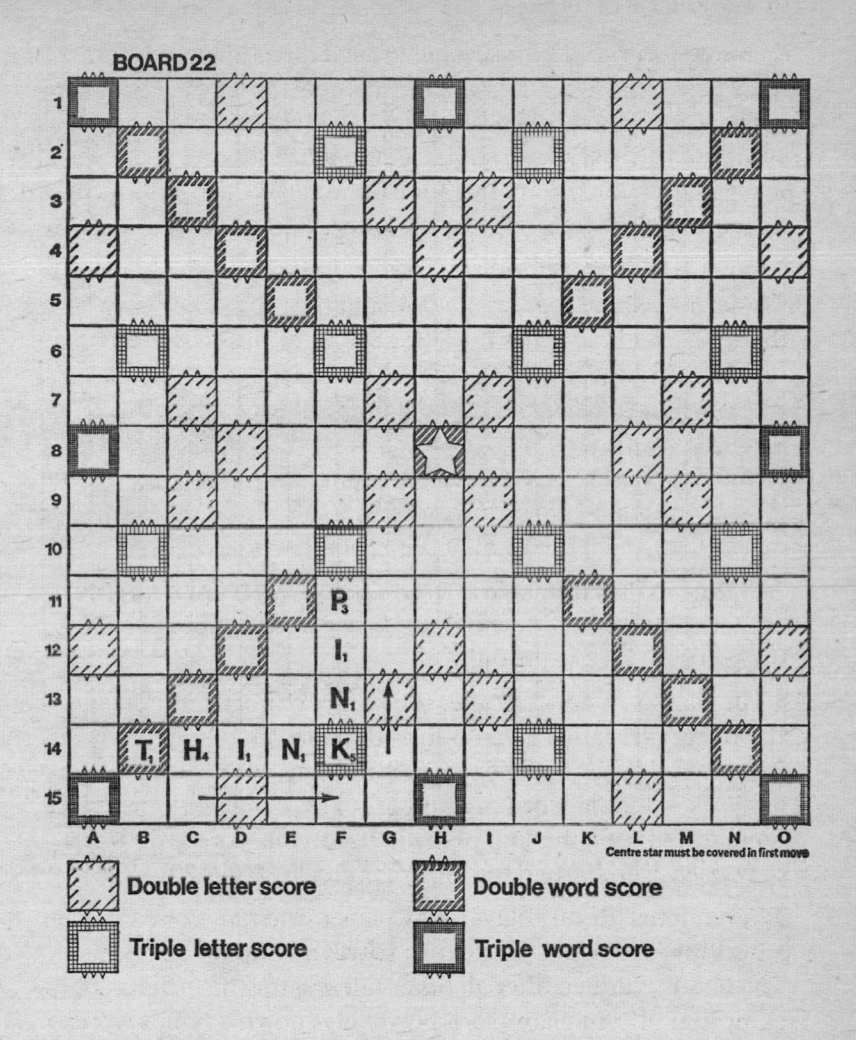

BOARD 22

Double letter score

Double word score

Triple letter score

Triple word score

Centre star must be covered in first move

A B C D E F G H I J K L M N O

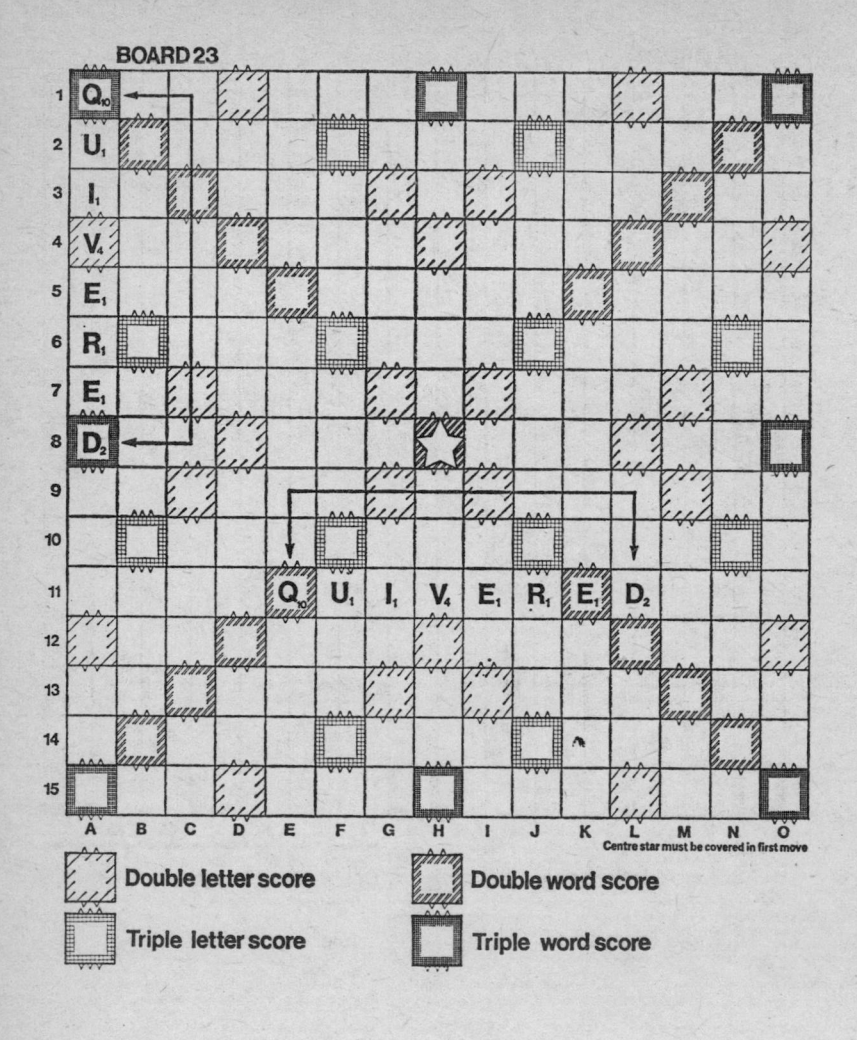

BOARD 23

	A	B	C	D	E	F	G	H	I	J	K	L	M	N	O
1	Q₁₀														
11					Q	U₁	I₁	V₄	E₁	R₁	E₁	D₂			

Double letter score

Double word score

Triple letter score

Triple word score

Centre star must be covered in first move

10 Final Scoring: At the end of the game each player's score is reduced by the total face values of tiles still in his hand. If one player has used all his letters, then his score is increased by the sum of the unplayed letters in his opponents' racks. A common ending variation is for players not to deduct the residual tiles from their own scores, but for the player who goes out to increase his score by double the face values of the unplayed letters of all the other players.

11 The Winner: The player with the highest score wins the game.

3 Tournament Scrabble

It is only human nature when a person is playing – and consistently winning – at a game, for him or her to start looking further afield for fresh challenges and hoped-for victories. In that respect games are not so different from political or military thinking.

Scrabble is no exception. Hence tournament Scrabble.

Scrabble tournaments began with the British National Championships in 1971; they hit the United States in late 1973 and reached Australia in a small way in 1977, with several other countries in between.

The British National Scrabble Championships were born in Bristol Prison in 1971. Gyles Brandreth, an avid Scrabbler, Monopoly Champion and professional games inventor, was in the prison, not serving a sentence himself, but doing research for a book on penal reform. He noticed how popular Scrabble was among the inmates and, knowing it was also one of the Queen's favourite indoor games, realized for the first time that it was a game that ran the whole gamut of society: from Bristol Prison to Buckingham Palace.

Inspired by this sudden realization, he decided to launch a national contest and put a small ad. in the Personal Column of *The Times* asking anyone who might be interested in taking part in a Scrabble Championship to write to him. Within four days he had received over three thousand replies – though none from Bristol Prison or Buckingham Palace. (Despite this lack of royal recognition he did give Princess Anne a Travel Scrabble set as her wedding present.)

Now, by 1977, well over 20,000 people take part in the Championships each year. They come in all shapes and sizes, and from all walks of life, and the one thing they all seem to have in common is a passionate commitment to the game.

The first ever Scrabble tournament in New York in 1974 attracted 2,300 protagonists. They played off over 13 weeks and annual tile-fests are now being run in such diverse cities as Baltimore, Miami, Wilmington, Sacramento, Oakland, Dallas and Philadelphia.

In the United States there is now even such a thing as Professional Scrabble, which crops up in game houses like the Chess Center on Manhattan's West 72nd Street – a cut-throat gameland which attracts such hot Scrabble players as Frank Kuehnrich, the official New York champion in 1975.

The first ever 'down-under' national Scrabble tournament is being organized for 1978 by *The Sun* newspaper, and Australian Scrabblers will be battling to beat the clock and the dictionary all through the summer.

When you have hundreds of people playing in a tournament the rules need to be not only more strict but also impeccably clear – especially when it comes to such things as acceptable words and legal time limits per turn. For these reasons special tournament rules apply. The British Championships adhere more closely to the standard Scrabble rules than the American tournaments – for example, they do not penalize a challenger if his challenge fails – but all tournaments operate on similar principles.

The most drastic rule, and the hardest for dawdlers to get used to, is the time limit: two minutes per turn in British Championships, three minutes per turn in American and Australian rules.

In most tournaments, the time limit means that you have that long to make your move, or else you most forfeit your turn. There is no such thing as a 'time bank', such as that operated by Professional Scrabble players, whereby you could carry over unused time from one turn to help you on the next. In American and Australian tournaments, there is also a master clock, which allows only one uninterrupted hour per game, whereas in the British Championships each game is played to its close, with no overall time limit.

Most tournaments are organized in much the same way –

qualifying rounds, regional finals and semifinals, national finals – with a set time-limit, a chosen 'house' dictionary, an official umpire or tournament director, and so forth.

For example, to enter the British National Scrabble Championships you have to obtain a form entitling you to enter the Qualifying Round. All you have to do is play two games of Scrabble where you like and with whom you like, and note the dates, the moves, and the scores on the form, with the signatures of witnesses. The completed forms are then sent back to organizer Brandreth, who computes the scores and invites the 300 players with the highest scores to take part in one of five Regional Finals.

Regional Finalists play two games each, and the hundred players with the highest aggregate scores are then through to challenge each other in the National Finals in London. At the National Finals, invigilators sit at each of the fifty tables, to keep score and operate the timer; they can also challenge words played by either player (this is quite the reverse of American and Australian tournaments, where challenging is an important part of playing strategy, and only your opponent can challenge you). There is an official umpire, and the tournament is kept moving smoothly by organizer Brandreth and a team of helpers. Each Finalist plays three games, and the player with the highest aggregate score at the end of the day is declared Champion and wins the antique silver cup which can be kept for life.

American Tournament Scrabble is somewhat more cut-throat than the British Championship, with its harsher challenge rules and its relentless master clock. But wherever you play, the tense excitement of the Scrabble tournament table is a far cry from the gentle family game played by millions.

Scrabble inventor Alfred Butts has never played in a tournament and says he never will.

The idea of using the clock as a weapon appals him. 'That doesn't seem fair,' he told me. 'It doesn't seem like fun any more. I want to play for fun.'

If you, however, like the idea of Tournament Scrabble, you should know the following rules.

The following are the rules adhered to by players in Scrabble tournaments. The British National Championship rules are given first, with the rules of Tournament Scrabble in the United States and Australia listed second, where they differ, under each section.

1 To Start

a There should be 100 tiles in the set. Both players should count them and place the tiles in the tile bag. In tournament Scrabble a bag is always used. Tiles are never placed face down beside the board as permitted in the standard rules.

b Each player draws a tile to determine who gets the starting position. The player with the letter nearest the beginning of the alphabet has the first move. A blank supersedes all other letters, and a player who draws a blank outranks a player who draws an *A*.

c Both players must return the starting tile to the bag, which is then thoroughly shuffled by either or both players.

d The player who has won the start fills his rack with seven tiles from the bag. The process is immediately repeated by his opponent, and the game begins.

2 The Clock

a *British rules:* Players have a maximum of two minutes per move. The invigilator at each table controls the timer, and will tell players when they have had one and a half minutes and when their two minutes are up. There is no overall time limit: play continues until the game is finished.

a *American and Australian rules:* Players have a maximum of three minutes per move, and there is an overall time limit of sixty minutes per game. There are actually two clocks. The master clock, controlled by the tournament director, signals the beginning and end of each game and once started, runs uninterruptedly for the sixty minutes. The second clock is the three-minute timer on each table, which is controlled by the contestants. The tournament director starts the main clock as soon as the players have returned their starting tile to the bag and *before* they draw their first rack of seven letters.

b *British rules:* If a player must leave the table during a game (which rarely happens), play is suspended until he returns.

b *American and Australian rules:* The official clock cannot be stopped during a tournament. If a player must leave the table, he loses as many turns as it takes for him to return. His missed turns are recorded as 'pass' on the score sheet by a game monitor, who sits out his three-minute turns for him. His opponent continues to play his turns as they come round.

c The timer is started for the first player as soon as both players have drawn their original seven tiles. The timer is then reset at the start of each turn throughout the game.

d If a player finishes his move before his time-limit has expired, he immediately announces his score and the timer is returned to the start position for his opponent to commence his turn. Each turn is a 'clean slate', and a player cannot build up a 'time bank' by demanding unused time from a previous turn when the clocks runs out on his next turn.

e Any player who has not played a complete word on the board when his time runs out must remove any tiles placed and forfeit his turn. A pass is recorded on his score sheet.

3 The Dictionary

a *British rules:* The latest edition of the *Shorter Oxford English Dictionary* is used in the Championships. Any word found in this dictionary is permitted, *except* proper nouns, words commonly spelt with a capital letter, words designated in the dictionary as alien, foreign or obsolete, abbreviations, letter sounds and words requiring apostrophes or hyphens.

a *American rules:* The *Funk & Wagnalls Standard College Dictionary* (1973) is considered the word bible for American tournaments. Any word found in it is permitted, *except* capitalized words (including proper nouns), prefixes and suffixes standing alone, abbreviations, words not labelled in the dictionary as parts of speech, and words requiring apostrophes or hyphens. Foreign, archaic, colloquial, slang, obsolete and italicized words *are* acceptable, if found in the dictionary and not outlawed by the exceptions given. Letter sounds too *are* acceptable, where these are listed in *Funk & Wagnalls*. For example the letter *v* is listed as *vee*; when pluralized it becomes *vees*; both are acceptable.

b The dictionary lists comparatives and superlatives of adjectives, declensions of verbs, and plurals of nouns only where the transformation is doubtful or unusual, and for some longer words. Normal comparatives, superlatives, declensions and plurals will be accepted, even where not listed.

b *American rules:* As above, except that comparatives and superlatives of adjectives of two or more syllables will be accepted only if listed in *Funk & Wagnalls*.

c No player may consult the dictionary during a game, and no other reading material is permitted at the game table. During any dispute, the official umpire (or tournament director) and his staff will have sole access to dictionaries.

d The official umpire (in Britain) or the tournament director (in America and Australia) is final arbiter in all dictionary disputes. His decision is not subject to appeal.

4 The Challenge

a Once a player has completed his turn, his opponent may challenge any word, or words, that were formed on that play. He may not challenge a word in some other region of the board.

a *British rules:* The table invigilator may also challenge a word. This is not the case in American and Australian tournaments.

b The disputed word is written on a 'challenge slip', which is then passed to a tournament monitor who takes it to the judges' table, where the word's legitimacy is adjudicated. The decision is then relayed back to the players.

c *British rules:* If the disputed word is acceptable to the judges, the player receives full points for the turn and the game continues. There is no penalty for the challenger.

c *American and Australian rules:* If the challenge fails, the challenger forfeits a turn and enters a 'pass' on his score sheet.

d If the disputed word is unacceptable to the judges, the player removes the offending tiles from the board, forfeits the points he would have scored, and writes 'pass' on his score sheet. He does not get a chance for another word.

5 The Play

a The first player, if he chooses to take his turn, combines two or more tiles from his rack and places them on the board, vertically or horizontally, to form a word. One tile must cover the pink centre square with the star. For this he receives a double-word score. Diagonal words are prohibited.

b He then counts his score for the turn and announces it out loud, whereupon it is entered on his score sheet. Player 1 then draws as many fresh tiles as are necessary to restock his rack. This procedure is followed after every turn.

c Player 2 then adds one or more letters to those already on the board to form a new word or words. He must play his tiles in one row only, and must play his word either vertically or horizontally. Any new words must touch at least one tile already on the board, and wherever fresh tiles touch previously played words or letters, those combinations must make complete, acceptable words.

d New words may be built by adding a letter or letters to a word already on the board; by placing a word at right-angles to an existing word, making use of at least one letter already on the board; or by placing a word parallel to an existing word, providing the adjoining letters all form acceptable words.

e Players are not permitted to shift tiles once a word is on the board. The tournament umpire or director is arbiter in such disputes.

6 The Blanks

a A blank must be designated as a specific letter as soon as it is played, and it retains that designation for the rest of the game.

b *American or Australian rules:* If the tiles played with can appear to be blanks when upside down, it is the opponent's responsibility to turn over a played blank and check that it is genuine. If it is a fake, the player who used it must take back tiles played in that turn and record a 'pass'. If a false blank is detected later in the game, it remains on the board without penalty.

7 Tile Selection

a Newly selected tiles must be placed face down on the table beside the player's rack. The player then checks to make sure he has drawn the right number to bring his rack back up to seven tiles. If he has drawn too many, he informs his opponent, who then selects the excess at random from the upside down tiles, and returns the extras, sight unseen, to the bag.

8 Passing

a Any player may use his turn to exchange any or all of the tiles in his rack for fresh tiles from the bag. He does this by drawing the unwanted tiles from his rack and placing them face down on the table. Next he takes the same number of new tiles from the bag and places them face down on the table, without looking at them, while he checks he has drawn the right number. Then the new tiles are placed on the rack and the discarded ones, still face down, are returned to the bag, which is reshuffled. This operation constitutes a complete turn, and a player who passes may not touch the board or play a word during his passing turn.

b *British rules:* A player may pass to exchange tiles four times – and *four times only* – in a game. He may do this at any point in the game, even if there is only one tile left in the bag.

b *American and Australian rules:* A player may pass and exchange tiles at any point in the game, any number of times, provided that there are seven or more tiles left in the bag. Tile exchange is *prohibited* once this minimum is reached.

c It is not compulsory for a player to exchange tiles when passing. He may pass without changing his tiles whenever he wishes as part of the game strategy.

c *Australian and American rules:* However, if both players pass for three successive turns, the game is terminated (this has never happened yet in a British Championship final).

9 The Finish

a *British rules:* There is no overall time limit. Play continues until all the tiles have been drawn from the bag, and one of the players has gone out (used all his tiles), or until all possible plays have been made.

a *American and Australian rules:* The game can end in three ways. The players can use all the tiles, and one of them go out, as above; they can mutually agree to end the match if no more plays can be made; or the master clock can run out, having reached the sixty-minute time-limit. If there is a semi-completed word on the board at the finish signal, no points are awarded for that turn. If a player has just finished laying a word at the bell, he must restock his rack if there are tiles left in the bag, before the game ends.

10 Scoring

a The score for each turn is compiled by adding the sum of the letter values for all words formed or modified during the play plus any additional points for placing tiles on premium squares.

b Premium letter squares are scored as follows. The score of a *letter* is DOUBLED when it lands on a double-letter square, and TRIPLED when it lands on a triple-letter square.

c Premium *word* squares are scored as follows. The score for the entire WORD is DOUBLED when any of its letters placed in that turn, even the blank, lands on a double-word square, and TRIPLED for a triple-word square. If two tiles played in a word land on double-word squares, the total word score is DOUBLED and then REDOUBLED, for FOUR times the face value; or the word-score is TRIPLED and then RETRIPLED for NINE times the face value, if two triple-letter squares are played.

d The premium squares affect the score only in the turn in which they are first played. After that, letters covering premium squares are scored at face value only.

e In the scoring of a turn, all premiums for double- and triple-letter squares must be included *before* doubling or tripling the complete word score.

f When two or more words are formed in the same turn, each word is scored fully with the common letter being accounted for in each word. This applies to premium squares as well as standard squares.

g Any player who plays all of his seven tiles in a single turn receives a bonus of 50 points, which is added to his score for that turn *after* all the premiums have been totalled.

h After his turn each player announces his score and it is filled in on his score sheet. Each score is checked by the opponent, and the table invigilator, and at the end of the game all scores are checked and validated by the umpire (or director).

i At the end of the game, each player's score is reduced by the sum of his unplayed tiles (any tiles left in the bag are ignored). If one player has gone out, then (*British rules*) his score is increased by the sum of his opponent's unplayed tiles, or (under

American and Australian rules) his score is increased by double the total of his opponent's unplayed tiles, while his opponent's tally remains unchanged.

j The player with the highest score wins the game.

k *British rules:* In the event of a tie, the players are declared tied.

k *American and Australian rules:* In the event of a tie, the player with the best single word score is declared the winner.

PART 2
STRATEGY

4 The Start

If you play basic Scrabble, the start of each game is decided by pure luck: each player draws a sample tile, and the person with a letter closest to *A* wins the right to start the game.

There are only two rules controlling the start. The opener must use two or more letters in his opening word, and one of those letters must cover the star in the centre of the board. For hitting that star, the first player doubles his score for the turn.

There are more exciting starts, involving mandatorily longer words, and these are listed further on in the chapter on game variations.

Alfred Butts experimented a good deal on a starting position for his game and for a while preferred the top left-hand corner. 'I tried all kinds of things to try to get the best arrangement for the start,' he said. 'I went to the top left-hand corner of the board because when you make words, they run from left to right and from top to bottom. I tried a lot of things, but I have to admit that that one really didn't work as well,' he said.

When Jim Brunot took over the game to market it, he rejected all ideas of a floating start and fixed the 'go' square in the centre of the board. He made the star pink – like the double-word squares that crisscross the board – and he guaranteed a bonus for the starting player.

He also, however, cunningly rearranged the double-letter premium squares that guard the centre star, and if you have a close look at the board, you can see why the follow-up players often out-score the game opener despite his double-word bonus. By laying down any starting word of two letters, the kick-off player automatically exposes two double-letter scores – one above and one below his word or one on each side of his word.

If his word is three letters in length, he also exposes a triple-letter square. If it is four tiles in length, he exposes a double-word opportunity to the follow-up player. And if his opening word is five letters in length, a naïve starter can also become a pawn for the next player's raid on a triple-word score. A five-letter word run straight out from the centre star goes dangerously close to a triple-word square. The next player can add an ending like -*est* or -*ing* to the opener's own word and profit handsomely.

So you can see the start is selfishly important apart from the fact that the opening round of play determines whether a game is going to be an open, freewheeling one or a complicated, two- and three-letter word war of attrition.

Many starting players feel they have no control over the board and merely place their four-, five- or six-letter word across the middle of the board. The only decision they make is whether to let the word run vertically or horizontally.

There are, however, several things the player with the opening position can do to protect his lead and get the most out of his first-down advantage. The first thing to remember is that this time is the only time in the whole game when you can play your hand with total freedom. Just this once you don't have to worry about other people's letters on the board blocking your way or stunting your word growth. The board is clean. It is empty. It is yours.

It shouldn't be necessary to point this out, but a lot of players seem to have a fetish for tidiness and symmetry when starting a game. If they are starting with a five-letter word, they place it neatly smack in the middle of the board with one letter covering the centre star and two letters running out on either side. By doing this, they may be scoring imaginary points for neatness, but they are robbing themselves of points on the score sheet. For example, on Board 24, I start with the word *march*. Placed in the middle of the board, it hits no double-letter squares and gives me a score of 12, which is doubled as the starter's bonus for a final 24. If, however, as on Board 25, I start off-centre (from 8–*D* through 8–*H*), the letter *H* hits the centre star rather

BOARD 24

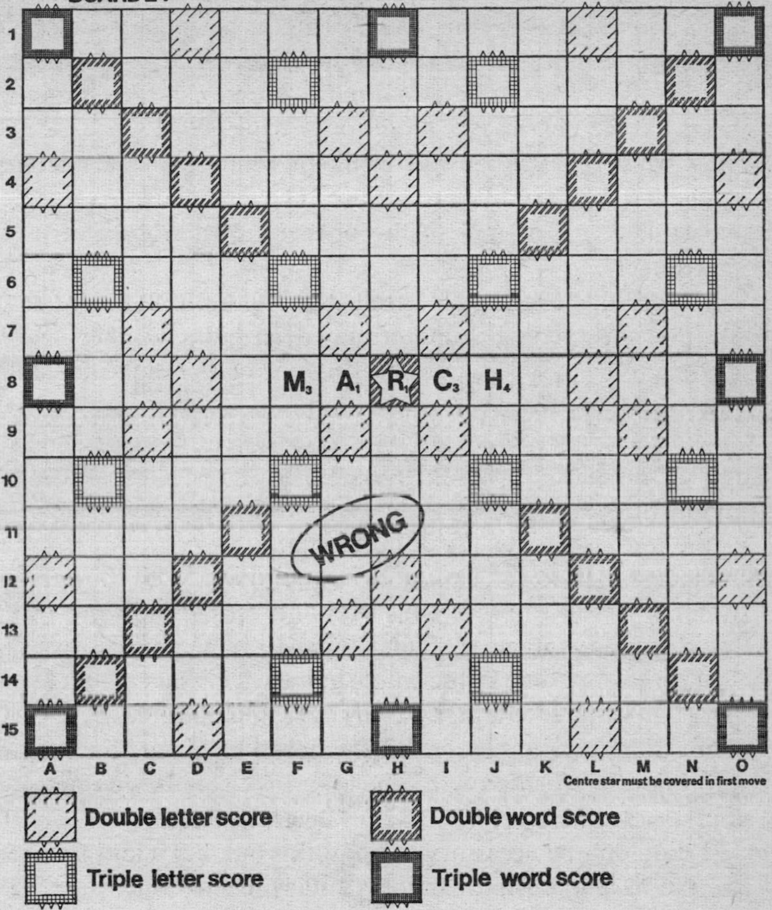
1
2
3
4
5
6
7
8
9
10
11
12
13
14
15
A B C D E F G H I J K L M N O
M3 A1 R1 C3 H4
WRONG
Centre star must be covered in first move
Double letter score
Double word score
Triple letter score
Triple word score

BOARD 25

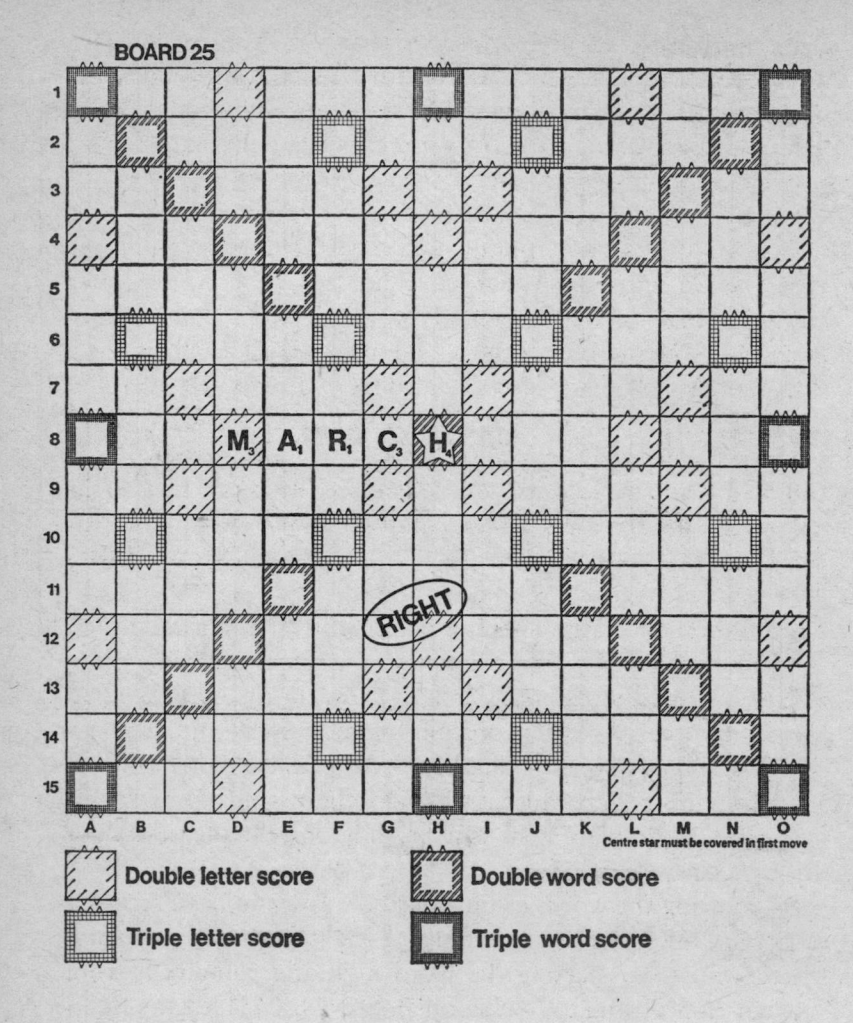

M₃ A₁ R₁ C₃ H₄

RIGHT

Centre star must be covered in first move

Double letter score

Double word score

Triple letter score

Triple word score

than the middle *R*, and my score is better. The *M* covers a double-letter square, which will be quadrupled by the end of the turn, and the 24 points become 30. Automatically, I reshuffle the letters before playing the word *march*, but the alternative word *charm* doesn't improve my score; so I settle for the 30.

'Aha,' says the alert student, 'if you had played the word *march* vertically or horizontally and started from the centre, the higher-value letter *H* would have landed on a double-letter square instead of the *M* and given you 2 more points, as in Board 26.' The sacrifice of these 2 points is what I call insurance. A five-letter word like *march*, started from the centre, takes you to within three tiles of a triple-word score. All the next player needs in order to go *marching* ahead of you are the tiles *I N G* and he hits the triple-word square and scores 48 points. It is far better to settle for the lower opening score and keep the triple-word square at a decent distance.

The importance of the opening placement of letters cannot be stressed too heavily. For example, in a lucky opening game recently, I had the letters *R X M T E E E* in my rack. We had agreed upon a five-letter word minimum to start, and after my opponent failed to open, I ran the word *extreme* down the board. I mention this play because it was a good example of how lucrative good letter placement can be, not only at the start, but throughout the game.

By centring the word, as on Board 27, I would have received 86 points (18 for the word, double for the start, 50 for the seven-letter bonus). By starting the word high and running it from squares *H*–3 through *H*–9, as on Board 28, I placed the high-scoring letter *X* on a double-letter square, giving it a total of 32 points of its own. The total score for the hand was 98 (24 for the word, double for the start, 50 for the bonus), an improvement of 12 points just from board management.

Also by starting high, I kept the word away from the bottom triple-word square. If I had started smack on the centre star, the word would have carried to within one tile of the triple-score square (*H*–15), and an opponent would have needed only an *S*

BOARD 26

Double letter score

Double word score

Triple letter score

Triple word score

Centre star must be covered in first move

BOARD 27

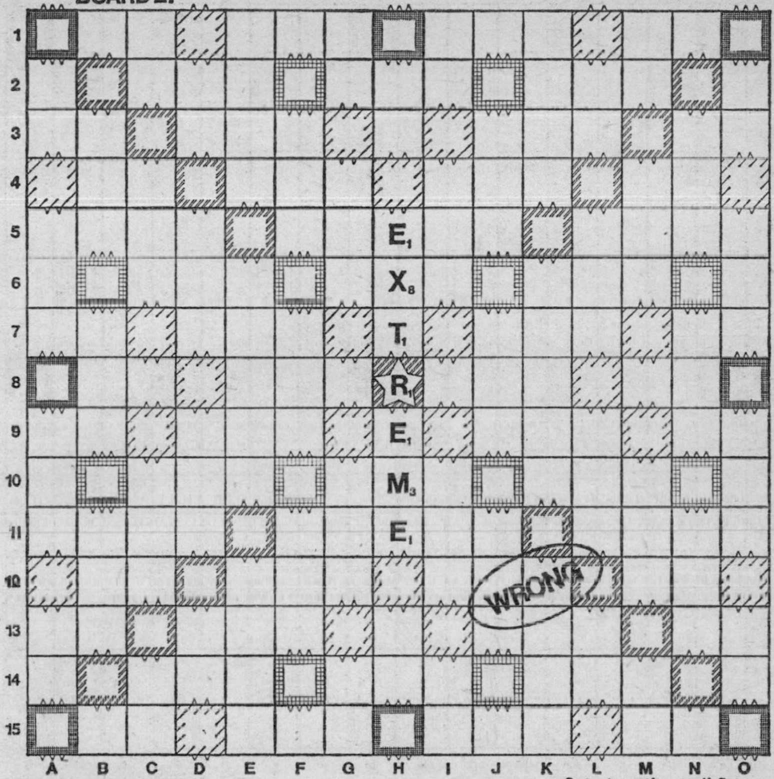

Centre star must be covered in first move

Double letter score

Double word score

Triple letter score

Triple word score

BOARD 28

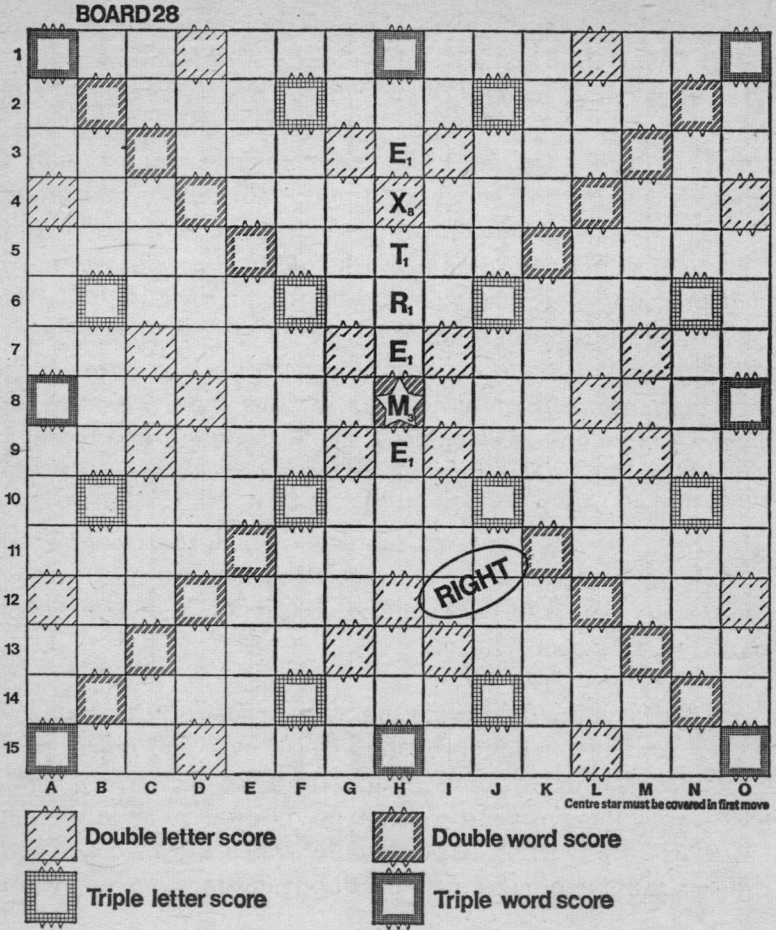

	Double letter score
	Double word score
	Triple letter score
	Triple word score

Centre star must be covered in first move

to make *extremes* and collect 51 points for lengthening my word, as on Board 29. Then if he added his own horizontal word, say *squaw*, worth 91 by itself, he would have had a total of 142 for the turn.

The score for the word *extreme* was high enough for me to break a starting rule: don't place vowels adjacent to the double-letter squares that surround the centre star. I mentioned earlier Brunot's cunning positioning of these premium squares. If, on your opening play, you place a vowel in squares *H*–7 or *H*–9 on a vertical word or on squares 8–*G* or 8–*I* on a horizontal word (Board 30), you make it easy for the next player to place a high-scoring consonant on either side of your exposed vowel and thereby double the face value of each consonant. It is better, if possible without crippling your own word, to put a vowel on the centre star and consonants on either side (Board 31) and increase the chance of your opponent's having to use low-scoring vowels on the double letter squares. In the case of the word *extreme*, it was better to break the rule and collect the bonanza for the strategically placed letter *X*.

One final starting tip. If your first rack of tiles is just a string of vowels and low-value consonants and the most you can get from a five-letter word is 5 points, doubled to 10 for the starting bonus, then seriously consider throwing in some or all of your tiles and drawing a fresh set. A 10-point score from a word stocked with vowels is only going to open the floodgates for your opponent.

BOARD 29

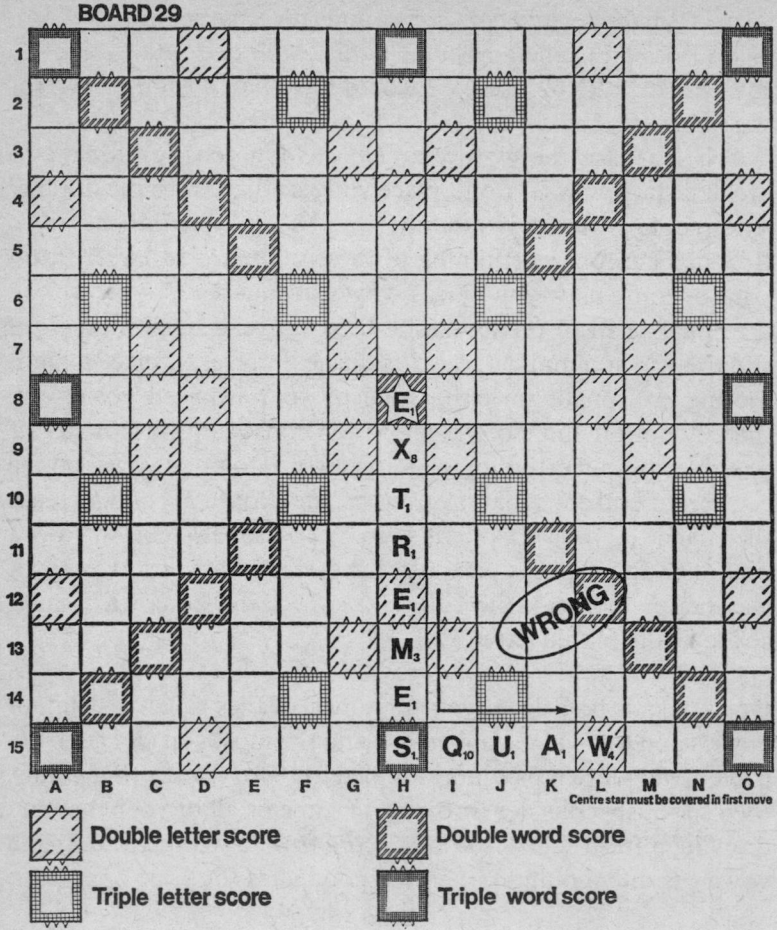

Centre star must be covered in first move

Double letter score

Double word score

Triple letter score

Triple word score

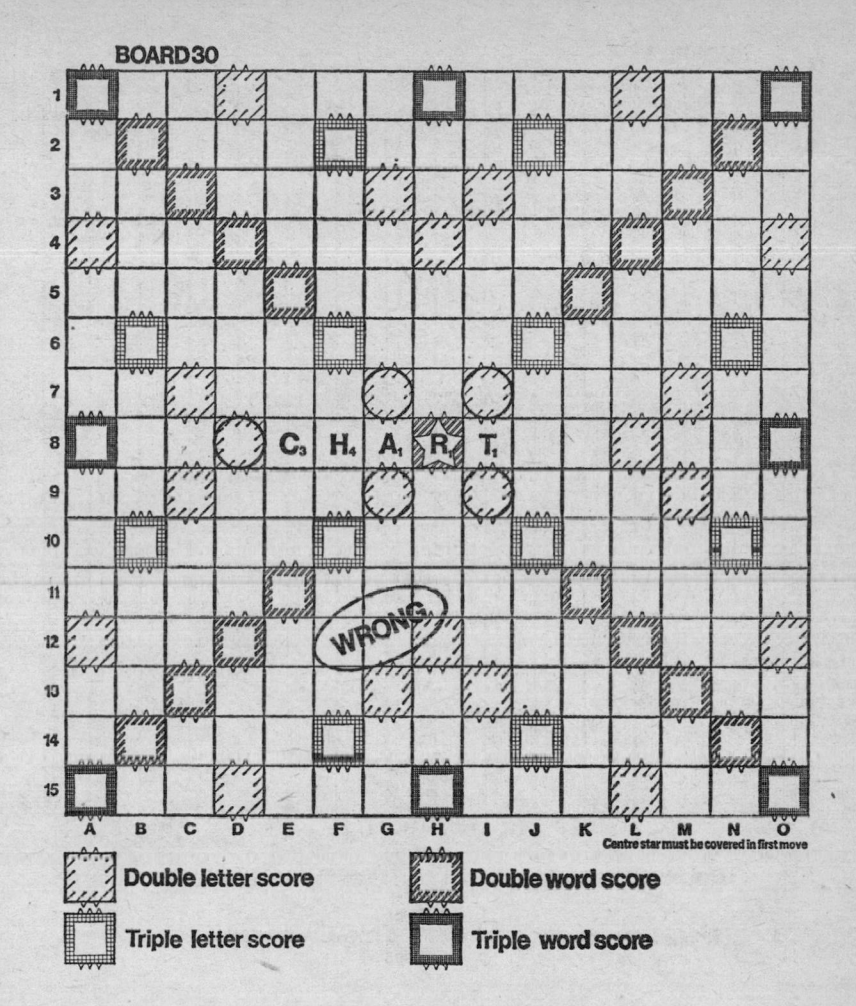

BOARD 30

Centre star must be covered in first move

Double letter score

Double word score

Triple letter score

Triple word score

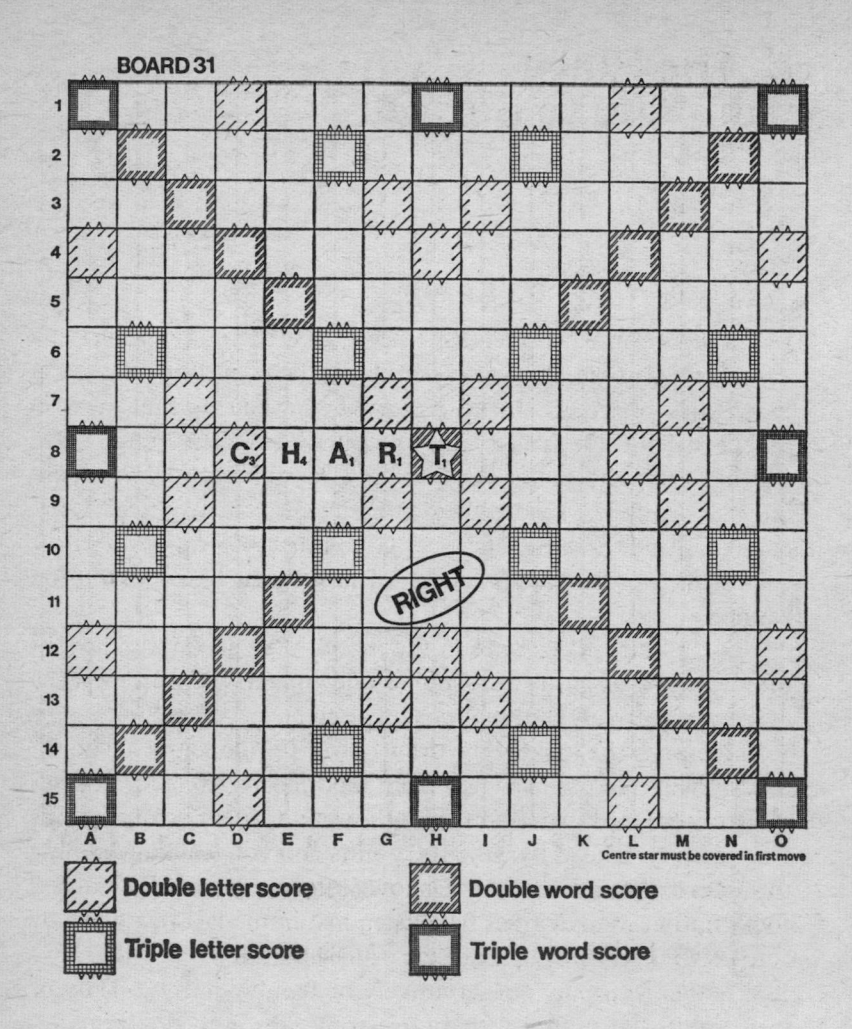

BOARD 31

Double letter score

Double word score

Triple letter score

Triple word score

Centre star must be covered in first move

5 The Play –
from Top to Bottom

By now it should be obvious, I hope, that there is more to this game of Scrabble than two people blithely putting tiles on a patchwork board. It is true, as I have said before, that the sole object in Scrabble is to plant your tiles across the board more skilfully and with better results than your competitor. But there are numerous ways you can do that. You can, from the start, play offensively or defensively; you can try to outsprint your opponent, or you can try to grind him down like a marathon runner.

You can also, if you are in the mood, play an unpopular but often victorious game as a spoiler and tighten the noose on the game so effectively that it almost expires.

Sometimes the luck of the draw or your opponent's luck and/or skill will make you switch from an offensive style to a defensive style in mid-game. On the other hand, there are occasions when you are ahead by, say, 100 points and you feel like opening the board up and making a showy run for home. Be warned though, that many games have been lost in the last few plays by smug leaders following that exact same course.

Whether you play conservatively or flamboyantly, openly or in a tightfisted manner, there are some absolute don'ts to remember. *Don't* open up a triple-word score square for your opponent. I'd like to say *never* do it, but there are exceptions, especially late in the game, when by doing it you get a decisive score of 50 or 70 and when all the high-scoring letters like the *Z*, *Q*, *X* and *J* have safely gone.

Also try to keep your big tiles away from double-word squares (unless your word covers it anyway). After all, you've drawn the high-scoring tile, so you should be the only one to get the benefit from it. Obviously, there's nothing worse than playing a word like *zeal* and getting very little for it and having your opponent come along to extend it to *zealot* in a way that just happens to reach a double- or triple-word score, and he runs away from you.

Another cardinal rule when playing with someone adept at making seven-letter bonus plays is to try to thwart his openings. Play words, if you can, that are past tenses of verbs that he can't add an *S* to for an easy hook to a seven-letter word. Or keep putting small two- and three-letter word hurdles in his way so that he can't get a clear run at seven empty squares. These are things you have to keep an eye on from the very first moves, and it is the style of those very first moves that sets the tone of the game. For example, on Board 32, the first player puts down the word *money*, played horizontally 8 *H–L* to score 28 points. By that positioning he leaves double-letter squares exposed on either side of the *O*, but goes for that position to collect 16 points for the letter *Y* on a double-letter score, redoubled because it is the opening play.

The second player, in this hypothetical game, has drawn poor letters, including a couple of low-scoring *N*s and a pair of *E*s. If this occurs later in the game, he should pass all seven letters and start anew, especially if all his tiles have face values of one point. This is expanded on in the passing strategy section later in the book.

But this early in the game Player 2, already nearly 30 points behind, is not keen to forfeit a turn and perhaps fall 60 or 70 points behind. In addition, by passing, he is giving his opponent a second unencumbered attack on the board, and the letter *M* is in a position that conceivably could be run out for a seven-letter bonus and a triple-word score. The letter *Y* from the word *money* is also sitting out there as an inviting tail on a double-word score play.

Player 2 makes a play that serves two purposes. He unloads four letters in a move that is called 'dumping' and therefore can replenish more than half of his rack without passing. And, more important, by a defensive placement he lassoes the board. The

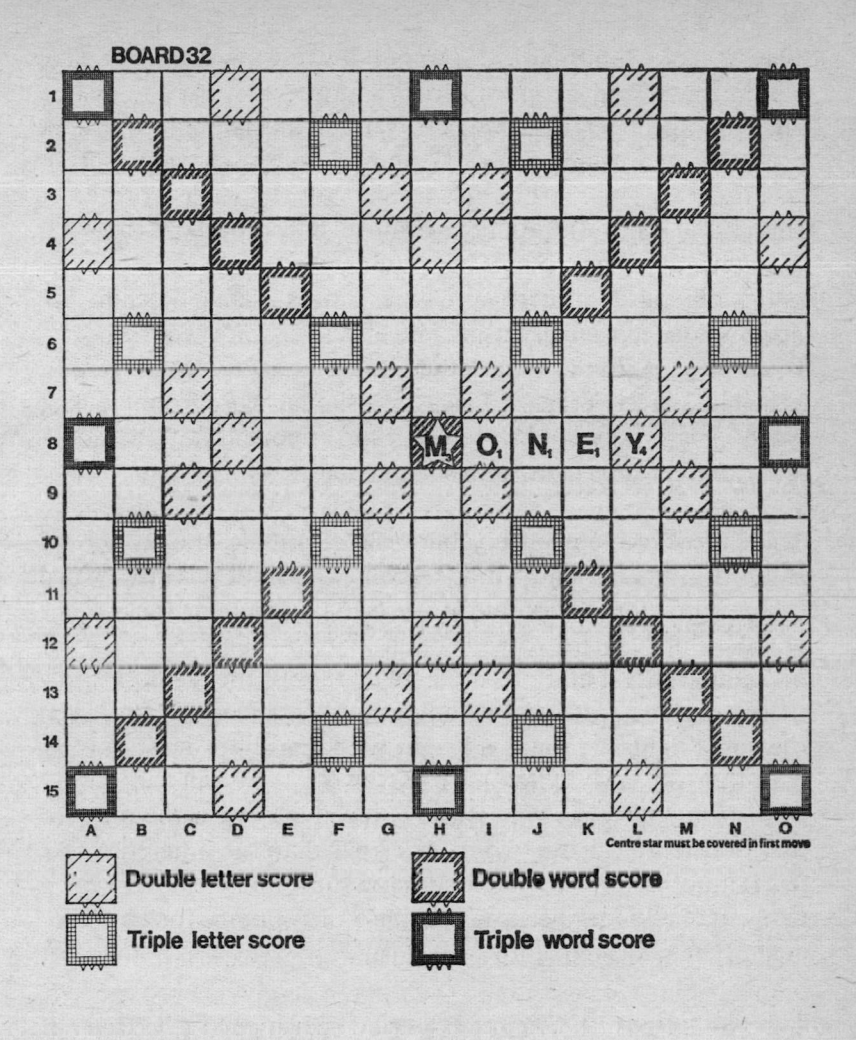

BOARD 32

Centre star must be covered in first move

Double letter score   Double word score

Triple letter score   Triple word score

play he makes on Board 33 is to put down the word *none*, and to tie up the board, he glues it to the previous word and runs it right along under the *O N E Y*. With that clamping move, he forms five words and scores 17 points. But, most important, he has used his low-scoring tiles to shut off the triple-word score threat and to foul up openings on several other lines and has managed to replace four of his tiles.

It is obvious that there were other moves available to him, but none unloaded as many tiles or so effectively blocked the board. In addition, with the same letters he could have been in trouble. If he had naïvely branched *none* or a similar word from the base word *money*, he would have given his opponent not one hook-letter, but a whole fisherman's haul (Board 34).

There are some people who abhor such Scrabble strategy. Alfred Butts, Jim Brunot and Tibor Urban (who until recently owned and manufactured Scrabble in Australia) are among them. They will develop a board so wide open that you can drive a Panzer division across it and not hit a single tile. Brunot said, 'I know there are a lot of players who like to play defensively and keep the game tight and that's all right with me. But I don't have to play that way. My wife and I played Scrabble right up to her death five years ago. We always enjoyed playing with an eye to the total score for the two of us rather than the difference of a few points between us. I still find that a more interesting approach to the game.' Does he expose triple-word squares for an opponent? 'Oh, yes. Frequently.'

The temptation to play expansively is great, and I'll admit to having been guilty of it myself. One urge to which players often succumb is to make a particularly clever word, usually one of those tricky, albeit low-scoring, ones that people don't think you have in your vocabulary.

Sometimes it turns out to be worth less than if the player had made judicious use of a single *M* or a *Y*. You'd be surprised how often the opportunity comes up in a game to put down a word like *my* or *em* or *ye* and land the *M* or *Y* on a triple-letter score.

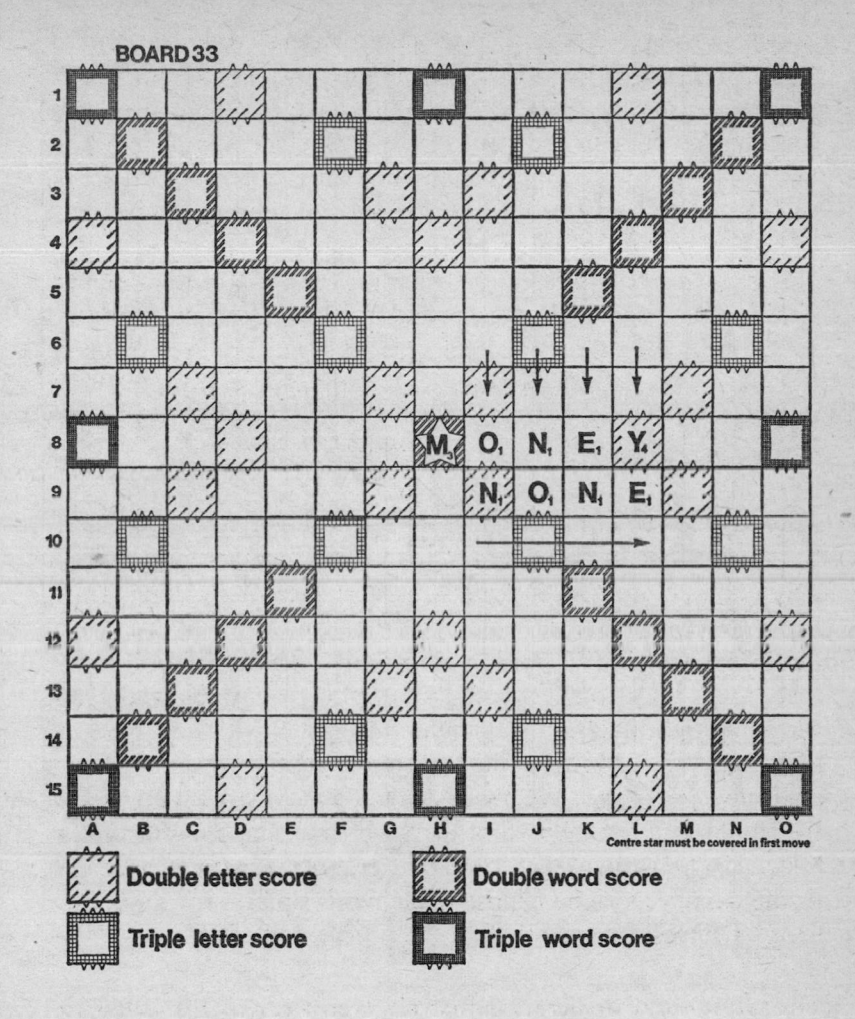

BOARD 33

Double letter score   Double word score

Triple letter score   Triple word score

Centre star must be covered in first move

BOARD 34

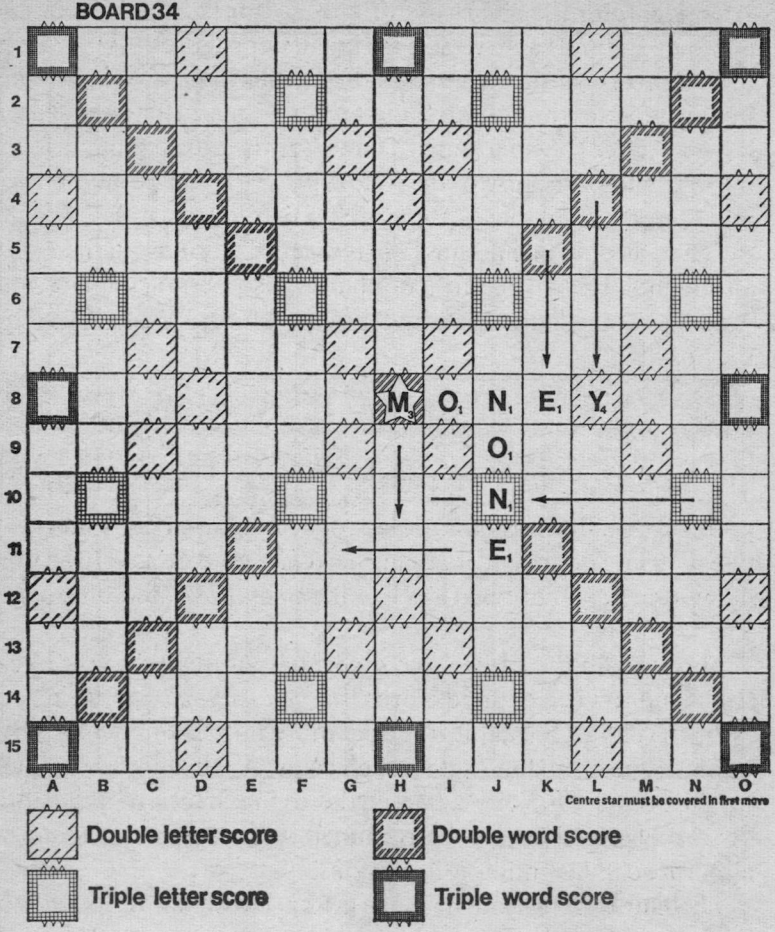

Centre star must be covered in first move

Double letter score   Double word score

Triple letter score   Triple word score

After all, with the smart use of a *Y*, it can be worth 24 point. alone – 12 going each way on a triple-letter square.

Which brings up the 'x-plosion' tactic. I think the *X* is my favourite letter, and as a two-letter humdinger I have called on it many times to win a game. To me it is the most valuable letter of the big four because of the following quirk: There are no two-letter words using the *Z*. There are no two-letter words using the *Q*. There is only one permissible two-letter word using the *J* (*jo*), although some American dictionaries also permit the word *ja*. That leaves the letter *X* worth 8 points before you even put it on the board.

It not only makes two-letter words when teamed with an *A* or an *E* or an *O* (*ax, ex, ox*) but it also – and this is the kicker – makes a two-letter word when the letter *I* is placed after it (*xi*). That means the letter *X* has the potential of being worth 48 points if you drop it on a triple-letter square and get something like *ox* going down and *ax* going across. You'd be surprised how many times a situation arises like the ones illustrated on Boards 35 and 36.

Throughout the game it pays to watch for these chances like a hawk and to keep in mind words like *box, pax, pox, lox* and *zax*. Near the end of the game it is even more important, defensively, to make sure you don't set up such gems. A person who can pick up 48 points with one letter in the dying stages of a game is obviously somebody to be reckoned with, and you should be alert for such last-minute 'x-plosions'.

The same thing can be done at an effective, although less devastating, level with the letter *H*, which alone can be worth 24 points when teamed with vowels to make the words *ah, oh, ch, he, ho, ha* and *hi*.

I mentioned the *Y* previously. It can be teamed in this two-way, triple-letter bonanza with four other letters to make the words *ay, by, my* and *ye*. Besides being good scoring combinations, these letters also help tighten the board.

Sometimes two defensive players get into a Scrabble tussle that is something akin to 'Indian Wrestling'. Each exerts more and more pressure on the opponent by tightening the board, play

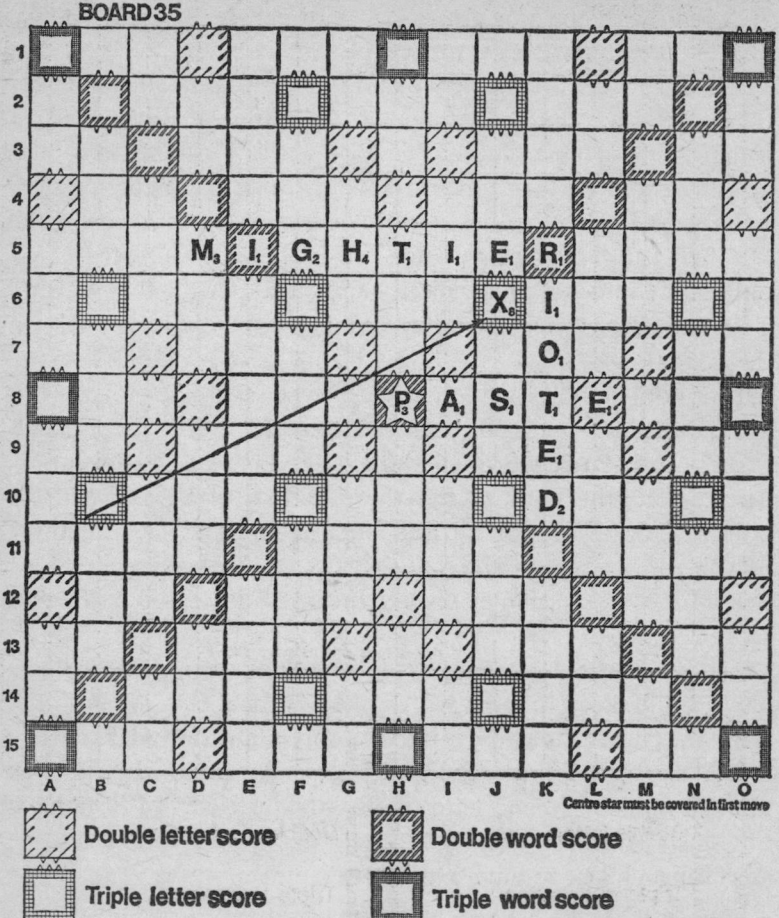

BOARD 35

Double letter score   Double word score

Triple letter score   Triple word score

Centre star must be covered in first move

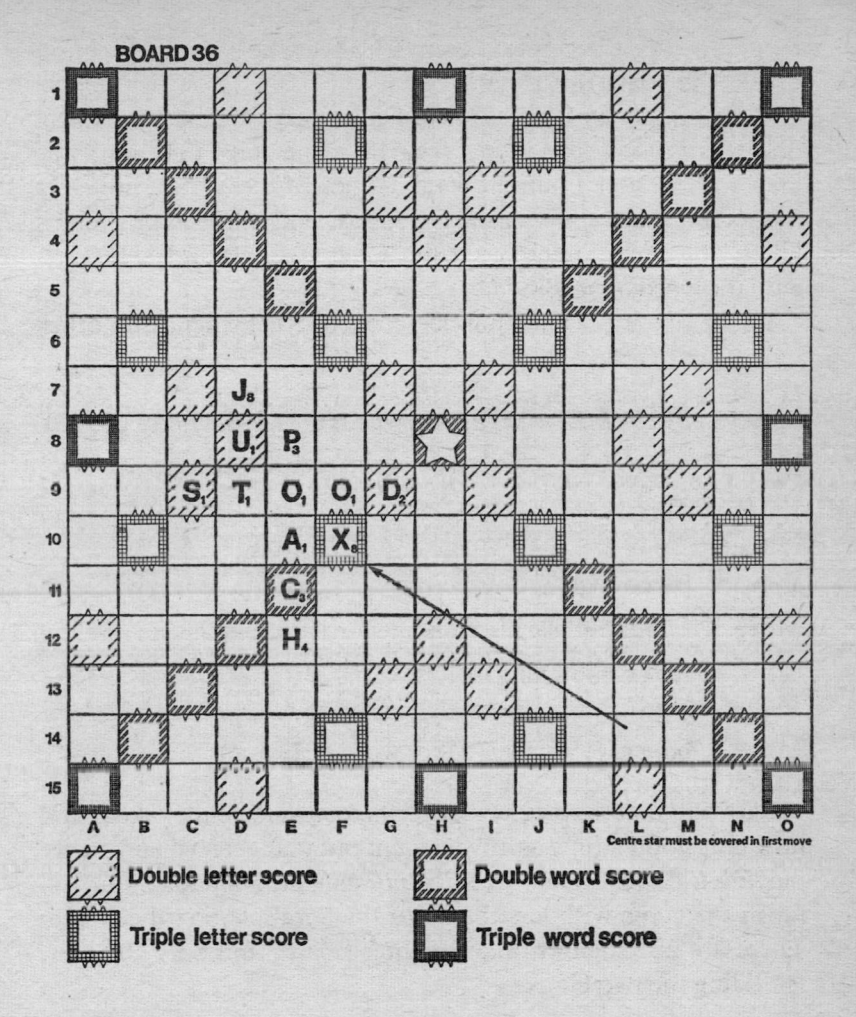

BOARD 36

Double letter score

Double word score

Triple letter score

Triple word score

Centre star must be covered in first move

by play, until it becomes a contest to see who submits first and breaks the board open again.

The example on Board 37 is not a very high-scoring one, but it does show how, turn after turn, the game stays tight until the area under attack is almost a solid block of tiles. There are eight moves in that small interlocking block, and unravelling them is like trying to undo one of those Chinese wood puzzles. It starts with the word *mate* (8 *G–J*).

Using the letter and number code to track them, the other moves are as follows:

Move 2 – *aye* (7 *I–K*); also makes words *at* (*I* 7–8) and *ye* (*J* 7–8)

Move 3 – *bar* (6 *I–K*); also makes words *bat* (*I* 6–8), *aye* (*J* 6–8) and *re* (*K* 6–7)

Move 4 – *red* (*K* 6–8); also makes word *mated* (8 *G–K*)

Move 5 – *payee* (*J* 5–9)

Move 6 – *aired* (*K* 4–8); also makes word *pi* (5 *J–K*)

Move 7 – *ten* (*L* 4–6); also makes words *at* (4 *K–L*), *pie* (5 *J–L*) and *barn* (6 *I–L*)

Move 8 – *bath* (*I* 6–9); also makes word *he* (9 *I–J*).

Play like that leaves the rest of the board looking naked, and now is as good a time as any to point out that even when you are playing the most open, free-flowing game imaginable, you still finish the game with less than half the Scrabble board covered. There are 225 squares on a Scrabble board, and only 100 tiles, including the two blanks.

To play a tight game it is imperative that you know at least some of the tricky two-letter words that are legal – words like *xi*, *na*, *em* and *en*. There are more than 60 of them listed in most dictionaries and a list of the generally accepted ones is given in the vocabulary section of this book. There are 69 of them in several American dictionaries and the full 13-volume Oxford permits such gems as *ut* and *ka*. The Concise Oxford doesn't.

It also pays, offensively or defensively, to have a good reper-

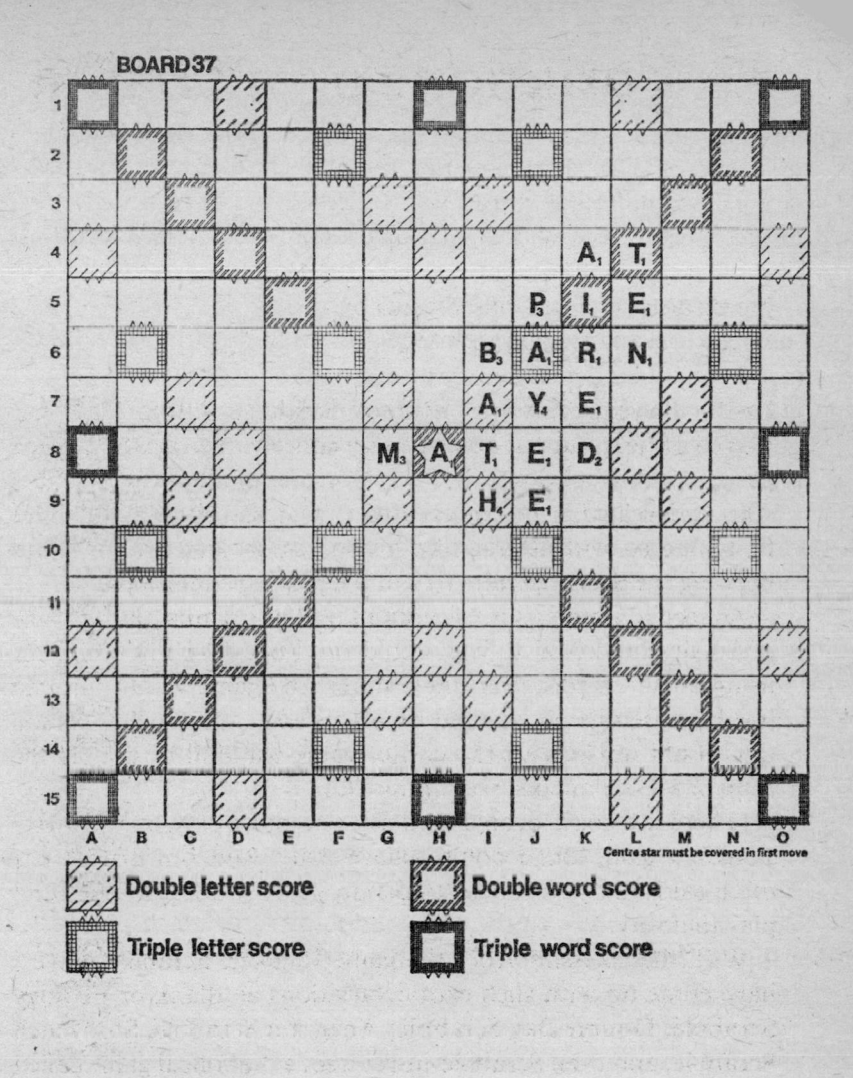

BOARD 37

Centre star must be covered in first move

Double letter score

Double word score

Triple letter score

Triple word score

e of tricky three-letter words like *mho*, *zax*, *ays* and *phi*. ese are also listed in the vocabulary section in the book. The big Oxford is a great temptation as an authoritative source because it lists other three-letter humdingers like *rax*. It also has, for example, the word *hadji* followed by 20 alternate or obsolete spellings. American dictionaries are even more eclectic. They have such three-letter gems as *haj* and *piu*.

Many good Scrabble plays are made by using the original word on the board and merely extending it to change its tense or inflection. For that reason, it is imperative to be always on the lookout for the option of adding -*ed*, -*ing*, -*iest*, -*er* or -*es* to an opponent's word.

You should also keep in mind the option of transforming a word by the use of prefixes like *inter*-, *re*-, *mis*- and *un*-, or by the addition of suffixes like -*ment*, -*ly*, -*able*, -*ness* or -*er*. This habit of top-and-tailing words is even more important when you are drawing a seeemingly endless supply of low-value tiles while your opponent keeps sucking up the big ones.

The experts say that luck has only a 12 per cent influence on the game, and it is true that a skilful player with poor tiles will often beat a lesser player who has drawn the greatest tiles in the set. However, that is slight consolation when you seem to have nothing but a roll call of one-point tiles on your rack.

The thing to do in such cases is to become proficient at word-bending – not only with the conjugation of verbs on the board or the declensions of nouns and adjectives, but by taking a word already on the board and by succinct addition of one or two tiles of your own, reap a harvest.

After a short time, some plays become obvious, such as expanding *zoo* into *zoon*, *jet* into *jets* or *jetted* and *qua* into *aqua*. But you can also get words like *kazoo* out of *zoo* and *jetty* and *jettison* from *jet* and *squat* and *quare* from *qua*. *Raze* can become *brazen*, *tamped* can be turned into a *stampede*, and so on. The big thing to remember is not to get discouraged if an opponent gets a word like *quiz* as on Board 38. There are oodles of retaliatory moves. A blank and an *ed* can give you *quizzed*, and you've

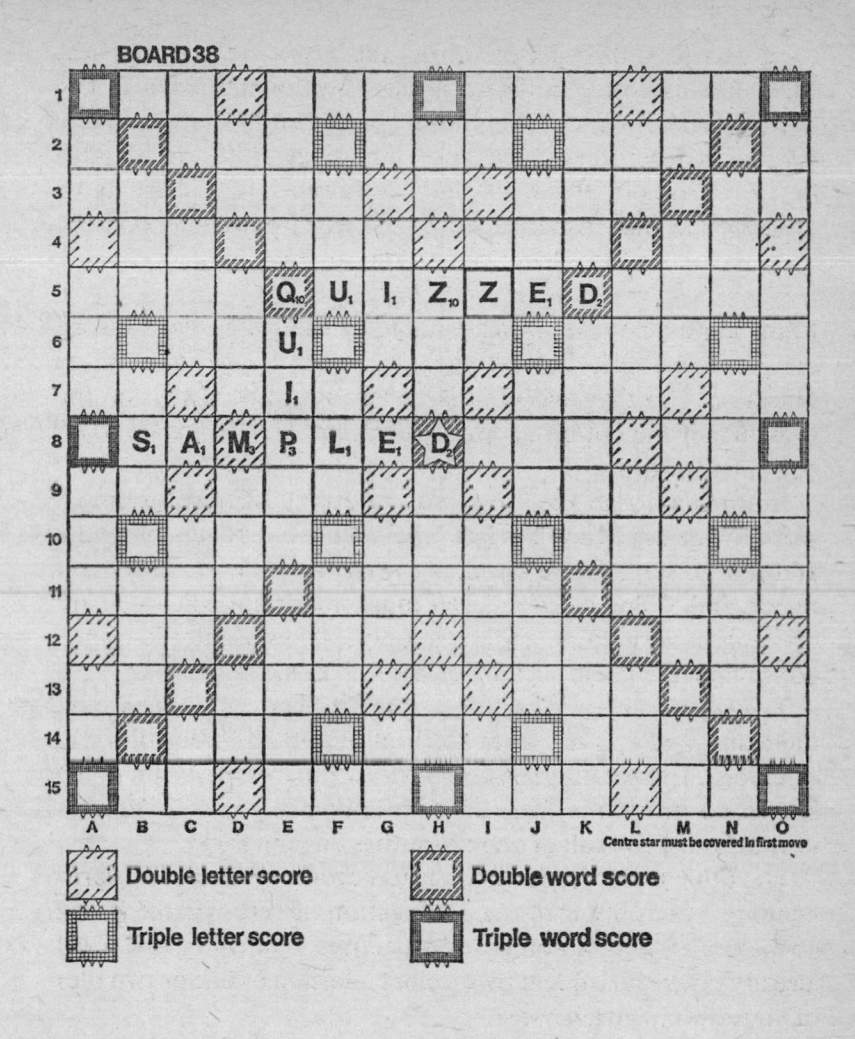

BOARD 38

Double letter score

Double word score

Triple letter score

Triple word score

Centre star must be covered in first move

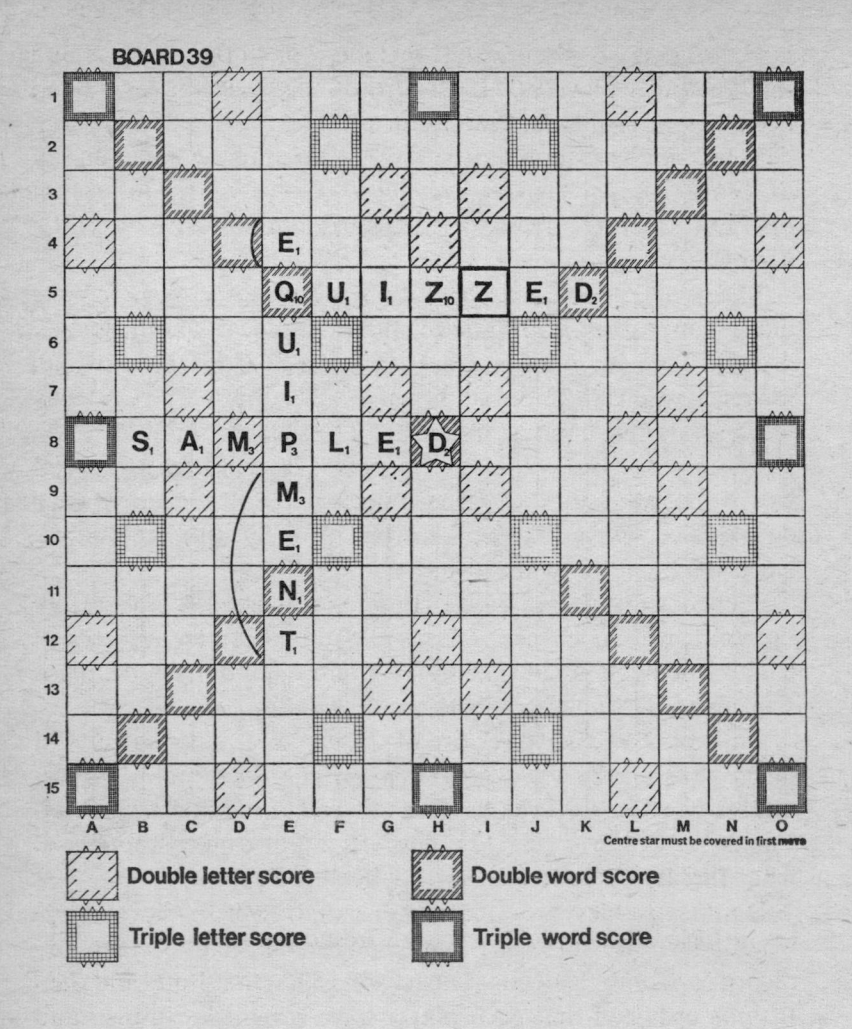

BOARD 39

Centre star must be covered in first move

Double letter score

Triple letter score

Double word score

Triple word score

got a double-word score that includes your opponent
the previously played *Q*. It's as if those high-scoring lette
been in your own hand for that turn.

Take another example (Board 39). You jump on either end
the word *quip* and make it *equipment*. Once again, you are not
only utilizing a *Q* already on the board, but you have also hit a
double-word score.

The point to remember is that a good player can often make
more from a high-scoring letter than the player who originally
drew it from the pool and put it on the board. On Board 38,
Player 1 received 22 points for *quiz* (an admittedly poor play
because, despite capitalizing on the *Q*, it did not land the *Z* on
a premium square). When the word was extended to *quizzed*, it
was worth 50 points. On Board 39, *quip*, with a double-word
count, was worth 30 points; extended to hit another double-
word square, it was worth 44 points.

Such extensions are more common when both players are
involved in a wide-open, offensive game and they are a great
leg up when you are at full stretch attempting to reach the high-
scoring double- and triple-word score squares.

On Board 40, the clever use of the exposed, innocuous word
tie gives a player the word *mightiest* for the capture of two
double-word score squares – what I call a 'double whammy'.
For this, the player gets 30 points (15 doubled) plus another 30
when the score is redoubled.

Double-doubles are uncommon, and triple-triples ('triple
whammies') are rare, but they produce the highest scores on
record for Scrabble fiends. The reason is that first Butts and then
Brunot ordained that each player have seven tiles in his hand
and then placed the triple-word squares *eight* spaces apart. To
reach them, you have to have somebody's previously played tile
as a stepping stone. It is only through these triple-triple plays,
though, that you can get such mind-boggling scores as 200–350
in a single turn.

The record for a single word in the Butts household is held
by Nina Butts, who ran the word *quixotic* down the top right-
hand side of the board. She leapfrogged over the word *fox*,

BOARD 40

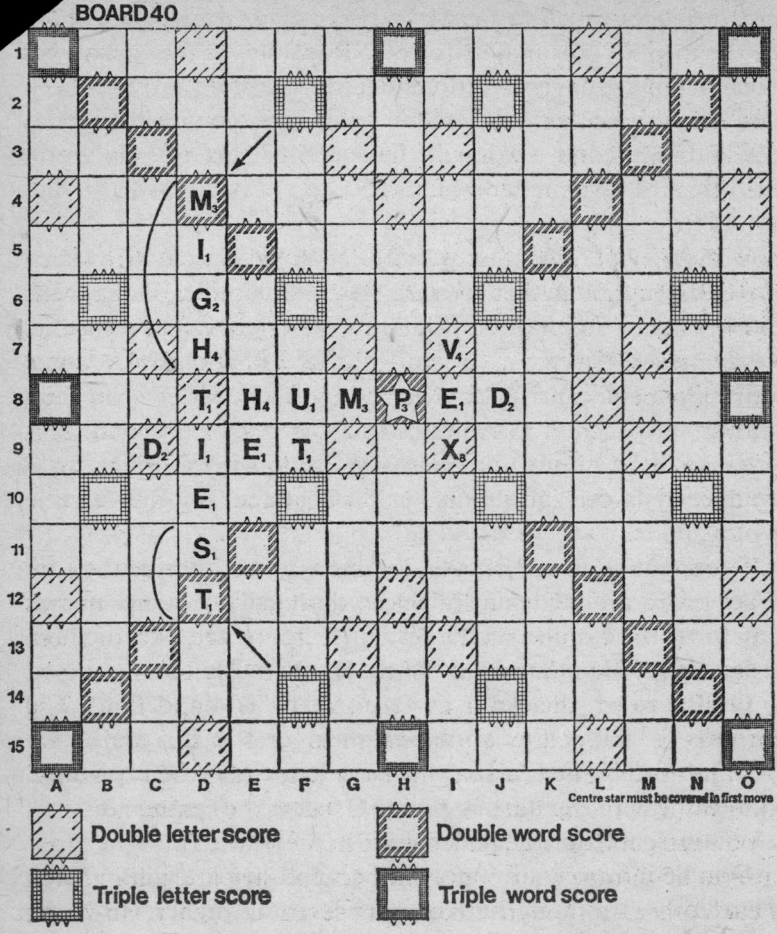

Centre star must be covered in first move

	Double letter score		Double word score
	Triple letter score		Triple word score

already played by her husband, and finished up with a score of 284 for the turn. Unfortunately for Mrs Butts, it was the *X* that was already in place covering a double-letter score. If the *X* had been hers and some other single-value letter had been on the line as the stepping stone, she could have scored 356 for the word, including the seven-letter bonus of 50.

You should guard against putting the stones in place for such moves. Even though they are rare, 'triple whammies' do happen; and when they do, they can 'whammy' you right out of the game. Never, never, never play a word like *raft* on Board 41, where your opponent can easily pick up one triple-letter score and without too much of a strain can reach across for a second. This obsession with double-doubles and triple-triples brings up a good, early-in-the-game strategy that I call the 'Big H and Little H ploy'.

If you look at Board 42, you will see that just outside the core of the board are strategically placed double-word score squares that form the outline of the letter *H*. There are two of these designs, the 'Big H' and the 'Little H'. The 'Big H' is outlined by double-word squares at *D*–4 and *D*–12, *L*–4 and *L*–12. The 'Little H' is outlined by double-word squares at *E*–5 and *E*–11, *K*–5 and *K*–11. The crossbar for each letter *H* is the horizontal middle line with the starting square's star in the centre.

You can get from one pink square in the 'Little H' to the other with no help from your opponent because they are within reach of each other – although a maximum seven tiles apart. However, if early in the game, and hopefully on his first move, your opponent makes that crossbar wide enough with a long, horizontal word, you need only six of your letters to go up three squares to the top of the goalpost and down three to the bottom to collect your 'double whammy'.

The fact that this is not achieved more often is because most shrewd starting players are conscious of such consequences and also because early in the game the area around the starting star is turbulent, unlike the eye of a hurricane. You'll usually find the region so littered that you can't get a clear run at both the top

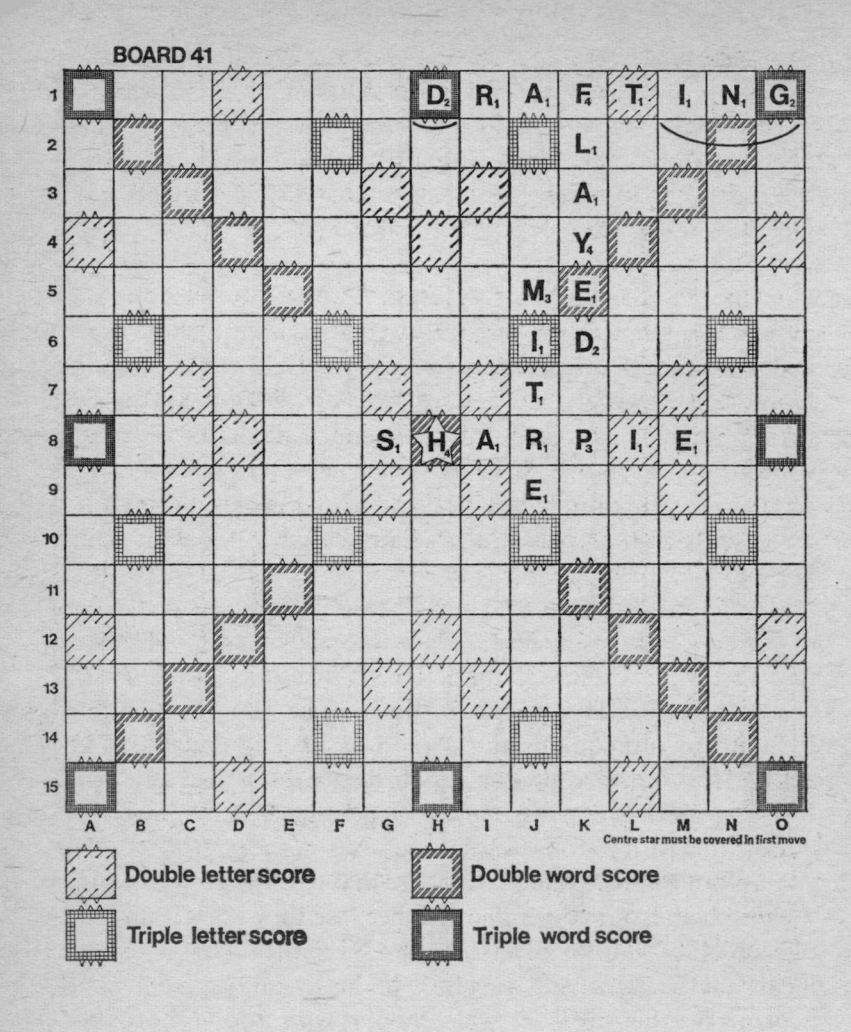

BOARD 41

Centre star must be covered in first move

Double letter score

Double word score

Triple letter score

Triple word score

BOARD 42

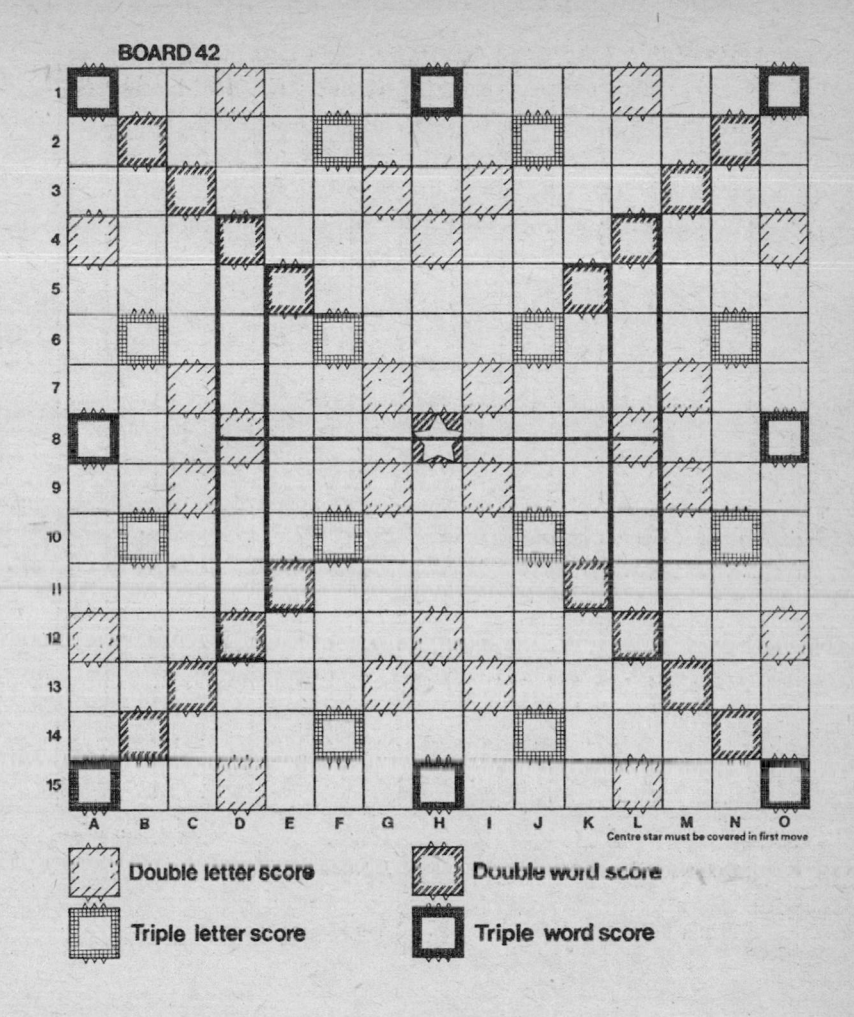

Centre star must be covered in first move

Double letter score

Double word score

Triple letter score

Triple word score

and the tail. To score on the 'Big H', you need some assistance because the two double-word squares are nine spaces apart, and you only have seven tiles.

Obviously, this assistance from an obliging opponent is not going to come your way often, but you'll be surprised how many times it does once you know about this ploy and once you start to envisage two Hs branded on the board.

6 Seven-letter Bonus Plays

In the past few pages I have moved up from talking about two- and three-letter words to seven-, eight- and nine-letter words stretching across the board.

It's time to talk about the seven-letter bonus.

The seven-letter play is to Scrabble what a hole-in-one is to a golfer. In some parts it's called a 'bingo', or a 'Scrabble', or even 'hitting the jackpot' – but whatever you call it, it's dramatic, it's gratifying, it's highly rewarding, and it can wreck an opponent's morale – especially if you can dish them up to him back to back.

The only time I ever won a Scrabble game by concession was when my opponent quit after I drew charmed tiles and scored three seven-letter plays and two triple-word score plays in my first five moves. Apart from your actual score, using all seven tiles in your rack in one move is worth 50 bonus points, which meant in the game I just mentioned that I had 150 points before I really started counting.

The idea of a 50-point bonus for a seven-letter play was not in the rules of Scrabble as drawn up by Alfred Butts when the game was still called Criss-crossword. It was a fillip added by Jim Brunot when he took over the game, and it has proved to be one of the most exciting things in Scrabble. Apart from the obvious incentive for players to hunt through their tiles for seven-letter combinations, it has also given encouragement to players trapped with low-scoring tiles in their racks. A lot of seven-letter plays are scored by players whose seven tiles have a total face value of around 10 or 12. The bonus 50 gives added muscle to the score for that turn.

Anybody can, and should, score seven-letter bonuses, and I believe an average player should ring one up every game. Somehow, though, they can elude people for years.

While researching part of this book in Australia, I interviewed Tibor (Tee Are) Urban, the man who used to own the Scrabble name and manufacture the game there. He told me the wrenching story of one elderly couple who had been playing 'bingoless' Scrabble for years. 'They are old friends of mine, they're both about 80, and they have been playing Scrabble every day for 18 or 19 years. One day we were talking about laying down all seven tiles in one move. The wife told me that she'd heard about it but didn't believe it could be done. She said they had been playing all those years and not once had either of them put down all seven letters in one move.'

The couple challenged Urban to a game. On his first move he spread out a seven-letter word.

It is true that some people are more adept at unscrambling anagrams than others and are also geared more closely to exploiting letters already on the board that can be built upon for seven-letter breaks. Some players, especially tournament competitors, have six-letter 'key words' that they use as tools in building bonus words. I call it the 'satire syndrome' because one of those keys is the word *satire*.

The practice started a couple of years ago when somebody stumbled across the fact that the six letters comprising the word *satire* can be jumbled and scrambled with practically any other letter of the alphabet to make a seven-letter word. For the record, 16 of the 26 letters of the alphabet can be added to the letters in the word *satire* and can be transformed into more than 40 seven-letter words.

There are other popular key words, including *retina* and *santer* (which is not in itself a word), and a list of all the possible combinations from these trunks is included in the vocabulary section at the back of the book.

It is fairly predictable that any seven-letter play you make is going to include a lot of vowels. There are two reasons for this. First, although there are only five vowels and 21 consonants in the alphabet, the vowels account for 42 of the 100 tiles in the Scrabble set. The figure rises to 44 when the *Y* is used as a vowel.

Second, the most common form of bonus play is when you add three or four letters to the front of such word endings as *-ies*, *-ied*, *-iest*, *-ing*. Other recurring endings are *-ion*, *-tion*, *-tian*, *-cing*, *-able*, *-ment*. When these letter combinations fall into your rack, make sure you recognize them, separate them, and try to sort your remaining letters into a bonus-scoring word

Once you have a word, there's the problem of finding a place on the board to put it. A good opponent will at all times try to limit the exposure of 'hooks' onto which you can attach your seven letters. The easiest place to drop a seven-letter word is to plug it into an exposed *S*; so while you are building seven-letter words in your rack, it pays to lean toward words that pluralize easily with the standard *S* ending.

On the same plane, it also pays not to be complacent. Don't stop searching your hand for alternatives once a seven-letter word has materialized. For example, you have the letters *S E C P E R T* in your hand. They spell the word *respect*, and a lot of people, in the flush of success at building a bonus word, hunt no further. However, that same letter combination can be twisted to make the words *spectre* and *sceptre/scepter*, and by making that additional effort to find extra words you often discover that a higher-scoring letter, like the *P*, lands on a triple-letter square for nine points rather than a tile with a face value of one.

Also, by having these alternatives in your head, you'll find it much easier to find a trunk word on the board on which to hang your seven-letter play. (This habit of automatically reshuffling a completed word to check out alternatives should also be applied to shorter words, and a list of good 'switch-hitters' is given in the vocabulary section.)

The two best tiles for seven-letter words are the same ones that are regarded as prize assets in other categories of the game. They are the letter *S* and the blank. The *S* is the most obliging letter in the game except for the chameleon blank, whether it be in your hand or on the table. If your opponent has left an exposed *S*, you can easily pin a seven-letter word right on it; and if he hasn't and you have one in your hand, you can usually find somewhere on the board a word that is just begging to be pluralized, as on Board 43. Then you not only get your word down, with its 50-point bonus, but you also get the face value of the word already on the board.

You'd be amazed what words can be pluralized – virtually any noun and, in some dictionaries, virtually any word. This often disputed theory is explained in detail in the vocabulary section.

The blank, as I said, is Scrabble's chameleon. It's a wild card, a joker, a free ticket, and nowhere is it more effective than in a bonus word. After a few games, you realize why, when passing tiles back into the pool, you never pass an *S* or a blank. Some good players follow an axiom that they never play the blank *except* as part of a seven-letter bonus. (The only exception is when they draw the *Q*, and all the *U* tiles are already on the board.) This is an extreme rule, unless you are a top-flight player, but it is good policy to milk the blank for all it is worth and never ever to regard it as a filler.

Some players, I have noticed, fall to pieces when they draw the blank. It's almost as if they can't cope with the freedom of having a tile to which they can attach whatever designation they choose. And I have often seen players, good players, totally come apart when they have been blessed with two blanks at the same time. The major problem, and this applies to most bonus play opportunities, is that players get locked into regarding the blank in limited terms. To them it is an extra *S* or, if they have the letters *I*, *N* in their rack, it automatically becomes a *G*. If they are holding an *R* or a *D*, the blank quickly becomes an *E* to make endings of *er* and *ed*.

These players limit their scope by not being adventurous enough, by not letting their minds picture the blank as any letter in the alphabet – even the *Z* and the *X* and the *Q*. Here's an example. In a recent game I was lucky enough to have a blank in hand along with the letters *R B A E I N*. I developed them into the word *brained* (using the blank as a *D*). This past tense verb was hard to place on the board – you can't pin the word *brained* onto an exposed *S*. Consciously bleaching the proxy *D* from my mind and letting the blank float pure and light, I found

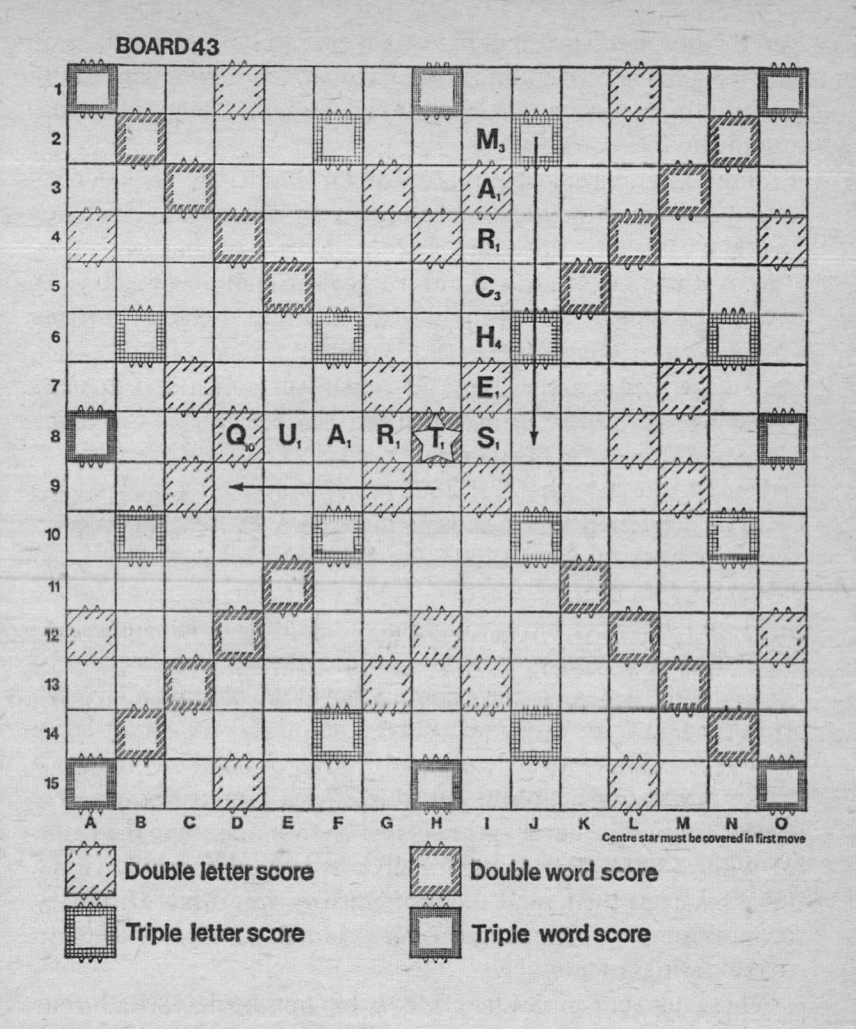

BOARD 43

Centre star must be covered in first move

Double letter score

Double word score

Triple letter score

Triple word score

it was only a matter of time before several other seven-letter words came up. The ultimate word was *bearing*, with the blank substituting for a *G*, and I managed to run it up the board off an *S* to hit a triple-word score.

Often the blank will become five or six different letters, in your head, that is, until you finally hit on something worthwhile. Another example: For some reason, I have trouble with the letter *C*. I dislike drawing it and try to dispose of it as quickly as I can. The letter *V* is not one of my favourites either. In one recent game, though, I drew the *C* with the letters *E L I A R* and a blank. By letting the blank float, I came up with *reclaim* (using it as an *M*), *glacier* (using it as a *G*) and *reliance* (using it as an *E*), with an *N* already on the board.

I mentioned good word endings that help in building bonus words, but when you are hunting for seven-letter giants, you should also keep in mind other good letter combinations like *th*, *ch, ph* and *ght*. It's a bit like building a prefabricated house – the more pieces you have precut and presized, the easier it is to build, especially if the pieces are as compatible in the basement as they are in the first-floor bedroom.

By now you are probably all set to get into a game and score five or six consecutive seven-letter plays. You should first read the following words of warning: bonus words are like hard drugs. Get a taste for them, and they can destroy you. I have become so obsessed by jackpot-hunting in a game that I have lost by more than 100 points.

It happens like this. You have letters in your hand that you just know are a mere trifle away from a 50-point bonus. The word just won't come; so you play away a couple of the letters – the ones you think are contaminating your rack and preventing you from making it. You hope the next letters you draw will make an easier bonus opportunity. Worse still, you pass and toss back one or two letters and draw anew in the dangerous game of 'fishing'. (When that works, it's magnificent. When it fails, it is horrendous. It is exactly like trying to fill an 'inside straight' in poker.)

Without your knowing it or even consciously agreeing to it, you are now totally committed to making a seven-letter word. While jockeying for position, you are falling behind, and suddenly it's a vicious circle. The more you hunt for a bonus word . . . the further you fall behind . . . the more imperative it becomes that you score a bonus . . . and the further you fall behind.

Finally, you get it. Jackpot. You collect your score and your 50-point bonus and discover that, after all the sweat and all those convolutions, your 80 points did not even make up the ground you lost over the preceding turns when you were jackpot-hunting and your opponent was romping over a virtually undefended board.

I have been guilty of deliberately squandering four turns for a grand total of 22 points because of a Machiavellian plot to set up and capitalize on a 'brilliant' seven-letter play. I put this in print in the hope that never again will I be tempted to repeat it.

There are two simple reasons why this bonus strategy is fraught with hazards. One is that the obsessed jackpot-hunter ends up playing against himself. Suddenly, consumed by 'jackpotitis', he ceases playing his opponent, and his inspection of the board becomes cursory. He is engrossed in a one-man bubble, just himself and his rack. It degenerates into a tussle between those pernicious tiles and his mind. The tiles often win.

The second reason that this sort of nonsense often fails is because the opponent knows immediately what you are doing. He doesn't have to be particularly observant to realize something strange is going on when a player who has been methodically scoring 35, 45 or 55 points in a turn suddenly puts down tiles that score 9, 6 and 7. The man has 'bonus-hunter' written all over him. Forewarned, the opponent picks away at the board, nailing letters like *W* and *Y* and *F* to triple-letter squares while making sure that each move tightens the board and that no move exposes an easy seven-letter word hook. As mentioned earlier, he can play words like past tenses of verbs ending in *ed* that cannot be pluralized, and he can also adroitly play words with letters like *C* and *V* in them.

These two letters (along with the *Z* and the *Q*) are the best defensive tiles in the pack. The reason is that there are no two-letter words starting with a *C* or a *V*, and there are no two-letter words ending in a *C* or a *V*. This is why you will often see a lone *C* tile holding back the tide as one-half of the board fills and the other half remains clear. I mentioned the *Z* and *Q* as being good defensive tiles because they, too, are immune from extension by adding a tile to make a two-letter word. However, these tiles carry such high face values that they are rarely used as blocking weapons.

One final thing to remember with seven-letter plays is that they are something like the elusive pot of gold at the end of the rainbow. Everybody knows they are there, but there are a thousand people who see or think they see a rainbow for every one who gets a piece of the gold. In this case, the gold is the 50-point bonus. But to put it in perspective, you should keep in mind that although a bonus play is worth 50 points for all seven letters, a single *X* can be worth 48 when played properly. That's only 2 points less, you've used six fewer letters, and you've also kept your ulcer quiet.

7 Rack Management

Throughout this section on Scrabble strategy, I have detailed how to score with such and-such a tile or how to score with a so-and-so combination. About now I can hear an exasperated chorus of 'okay for you to talk . . . you should see the tiles I get.'

It may come as a shock to some self-pitiers, but the tiles you end up with in your rack are often your own fault. The rack that says *I-I-I* or the one that looks like a train whistle going *T-O-O-O-T* has often been assembled through the player's own recklessness, stupidity, naïveté or a combination of all three.

It is true that you cannot be held responsible if you dip your hand in the tile pool and draw four tiles with the letter *A* on them and three with the letter *I*. You are guilty of a Scrabble offence, though, if you hold on to them through the next turn. You should sacrifice a turn and pass them back into the pool.

And you are also guilty if time and again you seem to end up with a rack full of vowels or seven straight consonants. There is a knack to keeping your tiles evenly seeded with vowels and consonants, and it is known to good players as 'rack balancing'.

The process of rack balancing is precisely what the name implies: keeping your rack equally balanced with vowels and consonants, because it is a rare word indeed that doesn't have a reasonable mix of both categories of letters. Ideally, you should try to keep a nearly equal mix of vowels and consonants in your rack at all times to give you maximum flexibility in word-building.

Good practice for this is to play inventor Butts's favourite Scrabble variation called 'Double Bag Scrabble', in which the vowels and consonants are kept in separate bags. That means that every single turn, when you go to replenish your rack, you have to make the decision as to whether your need for vowels is greater than your need for consonants.

Butts, who at one time unsuccessfully tried to convince Jim Brunot to have the tiles for vowels and consonants dyed different colours, noted that initially human greed gets the better of most players and they call heavily on the consonant bag. They end up with an impotent rack full of high-value, impressive-looking but unplayable consonants.

The cardinal rule in rack management is this. Don't play every hand as though it were your last. If you have the letters *W H Y I O U E* in your rack, don't play the word *why*. It may be the highest score available, but you'll be stripping your rack of consonants and leaving yourself open and vulnerable. You may find that at best it is impossible to form a good word on the next turn and you'll have to pass, or worse you'll have nothing with which to defend the board if the need arises. It is better in that play to make the word *you* or *hey* or even *hi* and suffer the lesser score until you can regroup.

Similarly, if your hand has five consonants and two vowels in it, don't play away the two vowels in a single turn. Keep one for insurance. For example, in your rack you have the tiles *E A W H Y P T*. You could unload four tiles in words such as *heap* or *hate* or *pate*, but that would leave you devoid of vowels. A far better move would be to play the word *paw*. It not only leaves a vowel in the residue, but also shapes your hand for a possible seven-letter play in the next turn.

This advance planning on bonus plays may seem ambitious, but it is a sound tactic to use, and good bonus players are endlessly trying to mould their racks into springboards for seven-letter plays.

By playing the word *heap* the sample hand was left with the tiles *W Y T*. This wasn't as bad as it could have been because the *Y* often saves a vowelless hand. But by sacrificing a few points and playing *paw*, the player's residue consisted of the tiles *E T H Y*, which are good seven-letter word starters – *th* being a good combination as well as *ty* and *thy*.

Another thing to watch for when attempting to maintain a well-balanced rack is the duplication of letters. Obviously, this will happen. You'll dive your hand into the tile pool in quest of two vowels, and you'll come up with two tiles each marked *L*. The thing to do in this case is to make sure you play one of those duplicated letters in your next turn.

Some people have the mistaken idea that your odds are somehow better for forming high-scoring words, especially seven-letter ones, if you have more than one of a kind in your rack. Perhaps it's a mind-fooler that if you only have to keep five or six different letters in your head, you can make a word more easily. It's not true. This isn't poker, and pairs you don't need. If you have a rack of tiles that includes two *L*s and, say, two *O*s, then obviously your range of word possibilities is gravely restricted.

As soon as you draw a duplicate letter, you must plot to unload it in your next turn. As long as duplications remain in your hand, your chances of seven-letter plays are diminished, and you are playing under an unnecessary handicap. There are only two exceptions to this rule. One is when you have more than one *S* in your hand, and the other is when you have both blank tiles. With that assistance, you should be able to play away all seven tiles in your next turn. A further hindrance when you have two of a kind in your rack is the crippling, but not uncommon, experience of drawing a third identical letter. When that happens, you are well up the street you don't talk about.

Some people follow house rules whereby if a player draws more than two of the same letter, he can reject all duplicates (over two) and redraw without penalty. (See the chapter on game variations.) My attitude is that if a person is caught with three of a kind, that's his problem, and he can try either to play them away or, more sensibly, forfeit a turn and attempt to recycle the offending letters when his next turn comes around. Usually, it is suicidal to try to hold grimly on and play away three or four tiles of the same letter. Often you fall much further behind than if you elect to miss one turn, and get rid of them all in one spring-clean.

If you do elect to play your way out of trouble, it pays to be well-stocked with good dumping words – especially ones that are full of low-value, duplicated vowels. Some of them have become stock dumping ground items in Scrabble. They are words like: *aal, voodoo, eerie, luau, miaow, cooee, adieu, audio, iota, queue, bureau, apogee, hoodoo, fiancee, radii* and *ratio*. There is a list of more than 50 good ones in the vocabulary section.

Another thing to keep in mind when you are balancing and manipulating your tiles is that, in one respect, Scrabble has a lot in common with card games like bridge, pinochle, gin rummy, whist and stud poker. You must keep track of the cards (in this case, tiles) that have already been played. It makes about as much sense for a Scrabble player to chase the word *exhaust* when both *H* tiles and both blanks have gone as it does for a card player to go for four kings when two of them are already exposed. It is too much to expect for players to keep a mental note on every tile in a game, but everybody can, and should, keep perpetual track of the major tiles.

To start with, you should know how many tiles of each letter are in the game. It doesn't take long to commit to memory the fact that there is only one *Z* and one *Q*, one *J* and one *X*. And after a few games, everybody knows there are four tiles with an *S* on them and two blanks. But you should also be aware that there are 12 *E* tiles and nine *A* tiles and nine *I* tiles. (The full list of tile distribution was given on page 18.)

Knowing when all tiles of a certain letter have been used can drastically alter a player's technique. For example, once the big guns have gone (the *Z Q X*), a player may gamble and risk exposing a triple-word score to his opponent providing his own score for that turn is a healthy one. The rationale is that with all the big ones out, and especially if most of the *H*s, *F*s, *W*s and the *K* are also on the board, the opponent cannot unleash a very damaging score even if he does seize the triple-word square on the next play.

By the same evaluation, a player with a late-in-the-game *S* feels much more secure about certain bold moves if he sees the other three *S* tiles on the board and if both blanks have also been neutralized. There is no way his competitor can pluralize most words for the remainder of the game, and, in addition, the opponent's chances for an eleventh hour seven-letter bonus are also greatly diminished.

There is one letter that every Scrabble player, from his early Scrabble days, gets into the habit of tracking with the tenacity of a bloodhound. That is the letter *U*. Each *U* is worth only one point, and there are only four of them, but they often prove to be the bane of many a Scrabble player's life. The reason is obvious: without one, you are usually stranded if you draw the *Q* tile from the bag. There are *U*-less *Q* words – like *cinq*, for example – but they are rare.

This quirk of the English language can cause ulcers, hair-pulling, nail biting and teeth-gnashing, and sometimes can make you wish you could just *QIT* (without a *U*). On occasions you seem to get all four *U*s in a game, but don't get a whiff of the *Q* – or you draw the *Q* early and then remain bereft of *U* tiles or blanks for the whole game.

Sometimes I feel that Butts or Brunot should have given the *Q* a higher face value than its current 10 points. Perhaps 15 or 20 to compensate for the risks you run by holding on to it. After all, if you draw a *Q* as your first letter in the game, you know you only have six chances (four *U*s and two blanks) of drawing a letter that can mate with it out of the remaining 99 tiles, and those odds aren't exactly enticing. In addition, as long as you hold on to the *Q*, awaiting the arrival of a *U*, you are virtually playing with a six-letter rack and are thwarted from even attempting a bonus play.

Because of this, a lot of good players who draw the *Q* early in the game will pass it back into the bag and forfeit a turn rather than carry its burden through future turns. This tactic especially makes sense if you can't get much of a score from your other tiles. It is also generally wise to pass the *Q* back into the bag in the middle of the game or the final third of the game if you draw it and two or more *U*s are already on the board. The imperative time to ditch it, even though you forfeit a turn and even if the game is close, is in a manoeuvre that I call the 'polecat pass'. That is when all *U*s and the blanks are out or when there is the bare minimum of tiles remaining in the pool and you don't have a blank or a *U* to match up with the *Q*. Your chances of being trapped with the *Q* at the end of the game (and thereby being penalized 20 points if your opponent goes out) are at this time somewhat substantial.

The other question is when do you play away a *U* in your hand and when do you hold it as insurance in case you draw the *Q*. I'll admit that I tend to hold a *U* back even though it leads to weak vowel combinations in the rack like *iu* and *au*. (The best vowel combinations, incidentally, are *ea*, *ai* and *ie*.) Sometimes – and I know this sounds unrealistic and lacking in logic – it depends on the 'feel' of the game. It's almost like in poker when you play a hunch and go for a straight rather than work on a safer hand.

Understandably, you are going to play a *U* if it is going to give you a massive score without waiting for the *Q*. Early in the game the risk of playing away a *U* is not that great because there is a fifty-fifty chance you won't draw the *Q* tile anyway. But for the final two-thirds of the game it *is* smart to hold on to a *U* until the *Q* has surfaced. A bonus from this is that if your opponent plays the *Q* you have a *U* of your own to build on his high-score letter.

If at any time you do play a *U* before the *Q* is out, make sure you play it in such a way that your opponent can't utilize it if he happens to be stranded with the *Q* in his hand. Play it up against the board walls or tucked in near other inhospitable letters, where it is safe and unplayable. Late in the game you can often tell whether or not your opponent has the letter *Q* by watching the expression on his face as you tuck a rare *U* in an unplayable spot.

This brings up another major point in rack management. Don't give yourself away by bad rack habits such as always putting the *Q* or the *Z* at the left-hand end of your rack or always keeping vowels at one end of the rack and consonants at the other. It's like playing pinochle or whist: you are a dead giveaway if you always keep your hearts at one end of your hand and spades at the other. I have seen a lot of players who might as well put their letters up in neon lights, judging by the way they flaunt the tiles on their racks. For example, don't automatically separate the tiles into words on your rack. If you have a five-letter word and two extra tiles, don't shunt the two letters to one end and leave the rack looking like 00 00000. It is much better to keep the seven tiles evenly spaced like so, 0 0 0 0 0 0 0, or break a seven-letter word like *tension* to look like *ten sion*. That is also a good safeguard if your opponent happens to get a glimpse of your letters. I have seen people who immediately send the *Q* to purgatory at the left end of the rack. The lineup looks like 0 000000, and an astute opponent can quickly guess what is going on. Sometimes, of course, it is a good idea to deliberately set up a phoney rack like that just to confuse him.

The appearance of your rack is especially important near the end of the game when you are down to your last seven tiles. If you think you can go out in three turns, don't break your rack up into a formation of 00 00 000. Break the tiles up in your mind, but keep them in an evenly spaced wall like 0 0 0 0 0 0 0. Of course, if the game is in its death throes and your letters are *Q Z X J K W H*, there's no harm in letting your opponent think you've got three smashing words in your rack. If that's the case, then by all means break them up into ostentatious groupings, such as *QZ XJKW H*.

And don't underestimate such psychological ploys. The following is more 'board management' than 'rack management', but as an experiment try the meaningful stare stunt. It goes like this. There's a great opening for a humdinger of a word on the bottom left corner of the board. You have a word organized in your rack, but it is your opponent's turn. What you do is shuffle your tiles feverishly and keep looking intently at the board – not at the bottom left corner, but at the top right. Your opponent is bound to note your agitation, and sometimes it will lure his attention to the area of the board that appears to have you captivated.

An extension of this is to look at a region of the board, as far removed as possible from where you hope to go next turn, and to make some remark like, 'That word *zloty* you played a coupie of turns ago was a terrific move. How many points was it worth again?' Or you say, 'When did you play the word *nester*? I'd have either challenged it or put an *S* on it if I'd seen it.' Both *zloty* and *nester*, of course, are pinned to a corner of the board far away from the area you hope to raid on your next turn, and a casual comment like that can sometimes just be enough to coax your opponent to a harmless area of the grid.

8 The Finishing Post

The final moves and manoeuvres in a Scrabble game are something that I relish – even when I am losing.

If you play cannily in the dying stages of a game, you'll be surprised how many times you can come from behind and steal a one- or two-point victory. And one of the most thrilling wins is when you can go out and catch your opponent with a handful of high-value tiles, and your bonus of double his residue of unplayed letters is just enough to beat him by a couple of points. I love it.

Inventor Butts and his wife, Nina, must have had some quiet, unexciting finishes to their games. They play a version in which no differentiation is made between the player who goes out and the one who is trapped with unplayed tiles. It makes no difference who finishes first . . . play continues until all the tiles have gone or until neither player can make a move. In other words, you may go out and seemingly catch your opponent with a bundle, but then he can leisurely pick away at the board in multiple turns until his tiles are exhausted.

Butts explained, 'We just keep playing until you can't play any more, and that's the end of it. This idea of counting the letters left when somebody goes out and you get double the score of the other players is absolutely silly to me. It's childish. It doesn't make any difference to the scores. You get two or three or four or five points. I don't think I've ever seen a game where it made any difference.'

That's not the case in my house. You catch somebody with a *J* in his hand, and it's worth 16 points to you, and that's not a bad score for a move in the final stages of a game. This is why end-of-game strategy is extremely important.

As the tiles dwindle in the pool, you must, more than ever, look ahead to future moves to ensure that you won't be caught with unplayable letters in the final turns. Rack-balancing rules still apply, but you have to improvise. Letters that were great defensive weapons early in the game, letters like the *C* and the *V*, are now liabilities. Their previous strengths, the fact that they cannot be used in two-letter words, now become their weaknesses, and you should try to play them away before you are down to your final seven letters.

Also, it is disaster to be caught in the final showdown with all vowels or all consonants. Actually, I believe it is worse in a close game to go into the final stretch with a hand heavy on vowels. That means you have all single-value tiles, and it becomes increasingly difficult to get any sort of competitive score in the final turns. A player with a hand weighted with consonants admittedly has trouble trying to go out, but he has the advantage of being able to place an *H* or a *W* for healthy, last-minute scores. Also, if you have seven vowels, it can take four or five turns to unload them all.

The thing to do is to shuffle and reshuffle your tiles and try to retain in your head as many word combinations as possible. Seven-letter plays are usually impossible at this stage, and often the board is so tight that only two- and three-letter word openings are available.

It is also inevitable at this stage of the game that your opponent is hunting as desperately as you are for openings, so it is not sufficient to spot one place where you can go and then blithely wait for your next turn to claim it. The odds are overwhelming that your opponent will grab it. If you have a word, keep poring over the board to see if you can find two or three or four places where it can be lodged or where another letter combination can be placed.

The most important thing is to think ahead.

If you have the letters *C A P* in your hand and you also have a *U*, don't play the word *cap* – play the word *cup* because it will be easier later to place a solo *A* than a *U*. One time, though, when you don't do that is when all the tiles have gone and the

Q is still absent. The odds are good you can trap your opponent with the *Q*, prevent him from going out, and collect the 20-point penalty. Under those circumstances, you play your *U* where it can't be used. Or you hold on to it.

If another *U* cannot be accounted for, then it means your opponent is still holding the *Q* and a *U*. That usually means he has a dearth of vowels in his hand and can't get a word down. Don't oblige him by opening up a chance where he can build on your vowels and get rid of his *Q* and his *U*. If you can, keep blocking the game up and picking away until all your seven tiles have gone.

You can see that keeping track of what letters have gone becomes critical in the final stages. Some good players know exactly what their opponents are holding by keeping a mental ledger of what tiles are still out. For example, if the *K* has not been played, you haven't got it, and all tiles have been drawn, don't play a word like *in* if it can easily be extended to *ink* or *kin*. If the *J* is still missing, don't expose an *O*, which your opponent can extend to *jo*, and be especially careful that you don't expose that letter below a triple-letter square where the *J* alone is worth 24 points.

You just have to know at this stage if all the big letters have gone as well as the four *S* tiles and the blanks. If a blank or an *S* is still unaccounted for, then look around the board and see if you have any high-scoring words still available for pluralization.

If the word *question*, for example, is on the board and you haven't got an *S* or a blank to use to pluralize it yourself, try to play a two-letter word off the exposed *N* so that it blocks the plural square even though it doesn't cover it. That sort of tactic, though, is for a defensive finish if you can't do anything scintillating yourself. The best finish is a strong burst where you catch your opponent with a rackful of tiles.

Ironically, there are times, when you are trailing, when it does not pay to go out. If all the big tiles are gone and you estimate your opponent has about 10 points left in his hand, it doesn't make much sense to go out if you are trailing by 50 points. In times like those, having apparently lost the game anyway, I have often stuck it out on the assumption that where there's life, there's hope. By hanging on and studying the board, you sometimes spot something, a gem that has been hidden there.

Or, as happened to me once, my opponent played the innocuous late-stage word *la*, which was close enough to a previously played *jug* for me to put a troublesome *U* in the middle and an *R* at the end to make the word *jugular*, which hit a double-word score. Suddenly I had 30 points to make it an evens race again.

That's what is great about this game. You can be trailing by 100 points and then maybe you get a couple of breaks . . . you draw the *X* and play it well . . . you win a challenge . . . your opponent passes . . . and his lead dissipates faster than a cup of hot water on the desert sand.

One of the dictionary definitions for the word *Scrabble* is 'to scrape together', and that's sometimes what you have to do to scrabble up a winning margin.

9 How and When to Challenge

True disputants are like sportsmen,
their whole delight is in the pursuit
ALEXANDER POPE, 1688–1744

Knowing when to challenge your opponent's use of words in Scrabble is a bit like knowing when somebody at your poker table is bluffing. Part of it is knowledge of the game, part is intuition, and part is pure gall.

The rules that deal with the sometimes embarrassing situation of accusing your opponent of cheating – or at least of being a prevaricator – are clear-cut. The standard Scrabble rules flatly state that any word formed on the board may be challenged before the start of the next player's turn.

The official rules for American Scrabble tournaments used to be a little more restrictive. They permitted a challenge of only one word played, or modified, in the previous turn, which meant that a shrewd player could drop an interlocking combination of letters that produced more than one disputed word, and it would be up to the challenger to decide which word was the most disputable. American and Australian Tournament Scrabble rules now state – and I believe this is a sound rule – that any word, formed or transformed in a single turn, is open to challenge. Under these tournament rules if a challenged word is ruled unacceptable, then the player responsible takes back the offending letters and misses his turn. If the challenged word is acceptable, according to whatever dictionary is being regarded as law, then the score for the hand stands, and the challenger misses a turn.

The British National Championships use the standard rules, the ones that are printed in the lids of Scrabble sets and are followed in many homes. They are less severe on challengers. The rules state that if a challenged word is rejected, then the guilty player takes back his tiles and loses his turn. There is *no* penalty to the challenger if the word is indeed in the dictionary. In other words, a player can challenge every single move by his opponent and keep him honest without ever risking any personal sacrifice.

At the other end of the scale is the variation of the challenge rule, which demands that whenever a player challenges a word, and loses, then he not only misses a turn, but his score is reduced by the amount that his opponent is legally entitled to for the play. That means that if the disputed word is worth 50 points, the instigator not only gets his 50 points, but his challenger loses 50 to make the play – in effect, a 100-point word. In my view, this is too punitive because it scares players away from challenges, even on preposterous words. You will also find, in a three- or four-handed game, that one player will sit back, let his opponents keep each other honest and bleed themselves to death, while he accepts everything without qualm and plays a parasitic winner's game.

There definitely are times when you should, as a cold-blooded tactic, permit an opponent's phoney word to stand unchallenged even though its presence may be aesthetically repugnant. For example, if your opponent puts down a nonword or a wrongly spelled word for which he gets 15 points and which as a result opens up a chance for you to make a seven-letter boardbuster worth 35 points plus a 50-point bonus, then for Heaven's sake don't challenge. Block your mind to pure English and proper spelling, and take the 85 points and run.

In a recent game my opponent hurriedly played the word *squirm* and, in her eagerness and playing with an upside-down board, spelled it without the letter *U*. It was late in the game, a close game that had been excruciatingly tight. Before challenging, I looked around and realized I could attach a seven-letter play to that phoney *sqirm*, which would hit a triple-word square and clinch the game. I let the spelling boob pass, took the 50-point bonus, won the game, and learned a lesson: Control all knee-jerk reactions to an opponent's spelling errors. You may be able to turn them to your own advantage.

Frank Kuehnrich, the New York City 1975 champion, is a defensive Scrabble player who confesses to being a 'heavy challenger'. After he won the title, Kuehnrich admitted to me, 'I challenge more than the average player . . . but it all depends. If I'm playing somebody with a big vocabulary, I won't challenge so much.'

Kuehnrich warned against a particular dangerous form of Scrabble player – the challenge fisherman. 'There are some players who are not so good, but they have a lot of words in their vocabulary, especially unusual words,' he said. 'They'll try to tempt you into a challenge that you'll lose, and then they will get an extra turn.' Such players will memorize words like *rabbet*. You challenge them, thinking they have made a spelling slip, only to discover they are one hop ahead of you. Your misspelled *rabbit* is a carpenter's term to describe a grooved piece of wood.

Another thing to remember if you are challenging is which dictionary is being used as the guideline. Scrabble tournament experts in America boast about the 69 two-letter words that are permissible in Funk & Wagnalls. They can dazzle you by spouting *aa, nu, mu, ex, ut, xi, wo, ka*. This tactic – and I have been guilty of it myself – can intimidate an opponent. Once the other player is convinced that you are an expert on two-letter words, then it doesn't take much to slip a phoney past him. For months, playing against my wife, I used the word *ra*. It is in one of the dictionaries, but it is capitalized and therefore illegal. And once somebody has lost a challenge on the word *ad*, which is a colloquial but legal word, according to the latest Oxford, it's not hard to twist his arm to get him to acquiesce on a word like *ed*, which is illegal.

One time you should always challenge is at the end of the game if your opponent is going out and if his word is even vaguely suspect. If you don't challenge, then the game is over anyway, so the last-ditch attempt to stop him costs you nothing. An opponent of mine went out in a game by playing the word *mont*. The game was close, and this was a desperate effort to get double the letter value of my remaining tiles and win the game. I had no idea whether or not *mont* was a word, but if I didn't challenge, the game was over. As it happened, there was no such word, the tiles were picked up, and the turn forfeited. I went out next turn and collected double the face value of the disputed *M O N* and *T*.

To muddy the waters further and make challenges more dangerous, different dictionaries have different standards. In the American dictionary Funk & Wagnalls, *ja*, the German for 'yes', is listed; on the other hand, the word *te* is not one of the 69 two-letter words permitted. The Concise Oxford however permits *te* but bans *ja*. In the full Oxford *ja* is listed as an obsolete form of the word *jay*. What it boils down to is knowing the pack of cards you are playing with, knowing your opponent's bluffing record, and knowing when to roll out a good old-fashioned, across-the-table, 'call me if you dare' stare-down.

And I challenge you to find a more exciting 'put your money where your mouth is' confrontation than that.

10 How and When to Pass

I don't think I've ever passed in a Scrabble game
ALFRED BUTTS

Despite Mr Butts's good fortune, one of the most important things to learn about Scrabble is to know when to pass – when to forfeit the chance to add something, anything, to your score and instead toss in some of your tiles in the hope of drawing a better selection.

The practice of passing is a strategem that has grown since the advent of competitive Scrabble and the growing importance of the 50-point bonus seven-letter words.

Before knowing when you should pass, you should know when you *may* pass. Under basic Scrabble rules, any player may use his turn to replace any of the seven letters in his rack. He does this by discarding the unwanted tiles face down on the table, draws an equal number of fresh tiles, mixes the discards with the remaining tiles in the pool, and awaits his next turn.

In those original rules, no provision was made for the player with a lucrative, but unplayable, seven-letter word combination in his hand, who is prepared to miss a turn in the hope that the board will open up for his next turn. The newer American and Australian tournament rules permit such passing without any exchange of tiles, but if both players pass three consecutive turns each, the game is terminated. House rules determine whether that means the game is scored as a draw, as in a chess stalemate, or whether the game should go to the person with the leading score. In the British National Championships, players may use their turn to exchange tiles only four times in a game.

The only restriction to passing is the stipulation made in

some house rules that there must still be at least seven tiles left in the tile pool. Once there are seven, or fewer, tiles in the pool, no passing of any kind is permitted. This restriction (not in the original rules) is necessary to thwart a player, caught with something like the *Q* late in the game, who tries to pass it back in when there is only one other tile in the pool. Without the seven-tile restriction, he could ditch it and keep passing until his opponent had drawn it. This restriction does not apply in the British Championships.

If a player elects to swap any or all of the tiles in his hand for a fresh supply from the pool, then that constitutes a complete turn. He is not permitted to place any tiles on the board or score in the same turn. Another variation permits any player caught with three or more of the same letter in his hand to discard the extra letters (in excess of two) and redraw without losing a turn. The exchange must be made immediately after the tiles are drawn.

So that's when you *can* pass; now when *should* you?

There's one cardinal rule: never pass unless you have to, and when you have to do it, then do it speedily and unflinchingly.

I always regard a pass as a 50-point penalty that sometimes has to be taken to shore up a crumbling position. The 50 points, in my mind, are made up by the 25-point score you could expect to get for a moderate play, and didn't, added to the minimum of 25 points you can expect your opponent to get during his bonus turn when you forfeit yours. Despite that, when I feel I have to revitalize my hand, I'll do it, and often the decision to pass can turn a game around in your favour.

The prime time to pass is when your hand is filled with duplicates, especially when it looks something like *U U I I N M L*. Obviously, you are not totally stumped with that hand, and you could play away some of the letters, but your score will probably be low and your rack still polluted.

I discussed earlier in this strategy section the importance of what Scrabble experts call 'rack balancing'. Sometimes, though, the bad luck of the draw and the game's development make it impossible to keep an equal number of vowels and consonants on hand. You are left with a set of tiles so unbalanced that the vowels are about to tip it over.

This is the time for drastic surgery. It's time to pass. There are special cases, but it is generally best to pass in all seven tiles when you are doing the spring-cleaning. Some people, though, play hunches and keep back a favourite letter or, if it's early in the game and you have both the *Q* and a *U*, you might want to keep both of them. With that pair, though, you should be able to play yourself out of trouble without passing.

To me it's a bit like five-card draw poker. Usually, if I have a good pair, I'll keep them and discard the other three cards for a redraw. But sometimes, if one of the other cards is a high one or if some inner voice speaks to me, I'll keep back a third 'floating' card. In Scrabble there are only two tiles that you absolutely must keep back when discarding on a pass. They are the *S* and the blank. These are the most versatile and, therefore, most valuable letters in the game and should never be discarded. It can be a dangerous game, but I will also sometimes keep back letter combinations like *ing* and *ion* because of the lure of seven-letter words with those letters.

The really dangerous game when passing, despite what I have just said, is fishing. That is when you have six great letters towards a possible seven-letter bonus and one tile that makes the proverbial fly in the ointment look harmless by comparison. The temptation is great to pass, throw back the offending letter, and 'fish' for a better one.

The temptation may be great, but the danger is even greater. Ask a poker player about the chances of trying to fill an 'inside straight' in poker. If you make it, you are a star, but if you miss, you have nothing. And, in fact, in both Scrabble and poker, you are far worse off than if you had gone for something less adventurous.

The risks of fishing are obviously affected by what you have in your hand – by what size hook you are using. Also, the decision on whether or not to fish is affected by whether or not you are winning and by how much.

I was trailing badly in a game and decided to go fishing because I urgently needed a bonus to give my score a transfusion. There were six great letters in my rack and one troublemaker, the *J*. The 'bait' letters were a blank and the tiles *O T I O N*. That lessened the risks while fishing. By treating the blank as an *S*, all I needed – to make a seven-letter word – was a *P* or an *M* or an *L* to make *potions*, *motions* or *lotions*. Reshuffling brought other possibilities – like using the blank as an *R* if I drew a *T* to make *tortion* or as a *T* if I drew an *R*. As it happened, I drew an *E* and used the blank as an *M* to make the word *emotion*. This was a case of fishing with an exceedingly large hook.

Another time to fish for a single letter is when your remaining six tiles make up one of those key words that will go with virtually any other letter of the alphabet to make a seven-letter word. Three of these, mentioned earlier, are *satire*, *retina* and *santer*, and Scrabble champion Frank Kuehnrich claims to have a few secret ones of his own.

If you have the word *satire* in your hand, it is important to know that 16 of the 26 letters in the alphabet can be added to some combination of those letters to make a bonus-scoring seven-letter word.

There are more than 40 seven-letter words possible (according to the Concise Oxford) if you start with *satire* as your six-letter base; they are listed in the vocabulary section of this book. With the word *retina*, at least 39 seven-letter words are possible when those six letters are mated in some combination with any of 16 other letters of the alphabet. The code word *santer* combines with 17 different letters of the alphabet to make at least 40 seven-letter words. Obviously, if you can memorize all, or some, of those words then fishing becomes a less dangerous sport. Even so, passing remains a serious tactic.

There is one late-in-the-game situation when it is imperative that you pass – providing you follow the rules (and there are still seven tiles remaining in the pool, if you are playing this rule).

This is the move mentioned before, that I call the 'polecat pass' because that's about as popular as it makes you.

Once again, it concerns the troublesome letter *Q*. If, near the game's end, you draw the *Q* and all the *U*s and both blanks have gone, you should treat it like a pariah. You must pass it back in. There is a chance you may draw it again, but it is a chance you have to take. As it stands, if you keep the *Q*, it is impossible for you to go out, and that makes your *Q* worth 20 points to your opponent if he goes out. At best, it will cost you a penalty of 10 points deducted from your total for being caught with it.

Sometimes you will find, when a hopeless-looking hand makes a pass seem inevitable, that you can salvage the turn by that low-scoring play called 'dumping'. By using this alternative method to revamp your hand – a strategy described in the chapter on rack management – you can unload several duplicated low-value tiles, pick up a few points, and avoid the stigma of having to forfeit a turn. There are good 'dumping words', and some are listed in the vocabulary section.

None of this, though, is as important as this simple rule about passing. When you feel you have to do it, then do it. Quickly. It's amazing the number of times you'll hear somebody cursing their luck and their poor tiles, and a bit later in the game they'll say, 'If only I'd passed way back when . . .'

The passing ploy in Scrabble is a bit like a visit to the dentist. Nobody can kid you that it's not going to hurt. But the longer you delay it, the more it will hurt – and not until the trouble is fixed can you smile again.

PART 3
SCRABBLING ABOUT

11 The Sneaky, Snide, Surreptitious, Swindling Scrabble Cheat

Anything worth having is worth cheating for
W. C. FIELDS

It may come as a shock to gentlemen players like Jim Brunot and Alfred Butts, but, like most games, Scrabble is not immune to the cheat. It's a sad fact of life that in any game where one person wins and one loses you are eventually going to run up against somebody trying to beat the odds, stack the pack, load the dice, get the edge, or inflate his score by cheating.

In Scrabble the cheat can be the white-haired grandmother, who supposedly can't see without her glasses, peeking while drawing her letters, or the sharp operator sneaking an upside-down tile on to the board and pretending it's a blank. Or it can be the student who never has trouble with the New Maths, but somehow always seems to botch the job when it comes to Scrabble scoring...

Hopefully, you won't be confronted by a cheat across your Scrabble table. If you are and if it is someone you cherish, then maybe it's best to shrug the whole thing off as an eccentricity or an oversight. The least you can do is to give him or her a chance to pass it off as an 'honest mistake'. However, if you are being ripped off by a board bandit, then at least you should be aware of some of the more insidious forms of Scrabble cheating.

Of course, if you haven't won a game in 20 years and have a criminal bent, then I suppose you could regard this chapter as a service -- a sort of do-it-yourself (illegally) Scrabble winner's kit.

The most common form of Scrabble cheating is the old 'looking in the tile bag trick' – the one attributed earlier to the allegedly shortsighted grandmother. It's surprising how many people are guilty of this illegality, and you'd also be surprised how many people dismiss it as an 'accident'. The game is going badly. The letters you grope for in the bag remain enticingly, infuriatingly out of reach. So you take a quick, almost accidental peep into the bag for a glimpse of your elusive desperately needed tile. When you spot it, your groping hand veers suddenly to that corner of the bag, and you lunge at the tile, with your hand behaving like one of those quaint, chain-operated cranes grabbing for prizes in the penny arcade. You can excuse such a lapse any way you like, but let's face it. That is cheating.

One way to prevent such tactics is to stick to the basic Scrabble rules governing the tile pool. Right at the start the rules state that the first thing you do is to turn all the tiles face down beside the board and shuffle them. Thereafter, the supply of tiles remains face down on the table, or in the lid of the Scrabble set, so that players must select their new tiles in full view of their opponents.

One drawback to keeping the tile reservoir upside down beside the board is the simple fact that the person who does the shuffling has a distinct advantage. Anybody with a reasonably retentive memory can remember approximately in what area he has seeded, say, the Z, Q and X. He can then make flamboyant shuffling gestures, with his hands agitating the tiles, without ever losing track of where the high-scoring tiles are stored.

If you don't believe that, then watch an expert shuffle dominoes. Even a good, albeit dishonest, domino shuffler can stir up a storm and still know exactly where the crucial double-six is lying. Because of this drawback, I adhere to the idea of using a bag to store the tiles. The bag I use is a hessian sack, which once held a bottle of Spanish sherry. It's a foot deep, and my wife sewed a drawstring ribbon into the neck. It is virtually cheat-proof because the only way you can see into it is to peer deliberately and fairly obviously down inside through a neck that is just wide enough to force a hand through.

Scrabble analysts claim that skill wins Scrabble games and that the luck of the draw constitutes only 12 per cent of the victory margin. Nevertheless, some people will do anything to eliminate even that 12 per cent, and that is why the second most common form of Scrabble cheating also involves tile selection. So be on the lookout for the 'cupped hand caper', an illegal procedure where a player plunges his hand into the tile bag and hauls out a cupped handful of tiles. He may be entitled to draw, say, three tiles, but by using his fingers as a shovel, he actually scoops six or seven tiles from the bag. The Scrabble cheat then quickly selects three tiles from the handful and drops the rest in the bag. In that one speedy motion, an accomplished cheat can select three desirable tiles that have surfaced face up in his cupped hand or, in a reverse action, can avoid letters that would duplicate tiles already in his hand.

The proper procedure is for each player to count each tile in his fingers while his hand is still hidden in the tile bag. He must then place each selected new tile *face down* beside his rack in full view of his opponent. Then he counts the number of new tiles to make sure he has drawn the correct number, and only then does he add them to his rack. If through a miscalculation, accidental or deliberate, a player winds up with more than seven tiles on his rack, he must immediately tell his opponent, who then blindly selects the excess tiles at random from the rack and returns them to the bag.

The overstocked hand is a tactic that all players should be alert for. A brazen cheat will deliberately overdraw letters when restocking his hand and then play with eight letters until he can make a seven-letter word to collect his 50-point bonus. What does he do with the extra letter? He palms it and drops it back in the pool when drawing his new supply of tiles. Or he keeps it and only draws six fresh letters instead of seven. If you think that is far-fetched, just think – when was the last time you counted the number of tiles in your opponent's rack? You just assumed he was playing with seven, right?

Another tactic of an adroit palmer is to exchange problem letters without forfeiting a turn by passing. This is done by surreptitiously hiding a problem letter in your hand after playing a normal turn. The unwanted letter is held in the palm and dropped back into the pool while the player is digging for new letters. A dishonest player who has laid out a three-letter word can palm an unwanted tile from his rack, drop it back in the pool, pick up four new letters (instead of the legal three), and usually escape detection.

In Monopoly the banker has more chances to cheat and more temptation to cheat because he's the player who handles the money. In Scrabble the same thing applies to the player who keeps the score. It's easy for him, especially if not playing against an eagle-eyed opponent, to trim a couple of points here and there from the competitor's tally. And by the same token he can occasionally pad his own score. Similarly, other players can steal a few bonus points by calling a double-letter as a triple or just by counting fast and with seeming authority while inflating the score for a turn.

The best way to overcome these temptations is for all players to keep score sheets and for each to add up his own and his opponent's scores. Besides keeping everybody honest, this is a good idea because psychologically it can give you a lift if every turn you can see the margin between you close (if you are fighting back from a losing streak) or widen (if you are pulling away). All players should also count the board score for each individual turn.

There is one board tactic that some people call cheating and others regard as mere messy play. That is the tactic whereby a player places a word on the board and then, after it is down, starts rearranging the letters. This is a no-no. I mention it because the real Scrabble cheat will often use such a ploy to get an edge on his opponent. Often by watching an opponent's face while placing a dubious word, a good cheat can gauge whether he is likely to be challenged or not. If the opponent has a real 'gotcha' look in his eye, then the cheater can swiftly rearrange his letters, on the board, to salvage a lower-scoring, but legal word.

And while we are on the subject of challenging and cheating, watch out for the dictionary browser – the person who under the guise of looking up a disputed word takes about 15 minutes to find it in the dictionary. He's the person who volunteers to look up a challenged word beginning with a *W* and starts looking for it under *J*. The next thing you know, he puts the word *jaggery* on the board for a big triple-word score plus a bonus of 50 and says, 'Oh, everybody knows what *jaggery* is. It's a coarse brown Indian sugar made from palm sap.' Of course 'everybody knows', especially if they have just spotted it in the dictionary.

By devoting so much space to dishonest Scrabble tactics, I hate to give the impression that the world is filled with tile tricksters and board bandits. Still, these things are worth knowing, so that if you do get beaten, at least you know you were beaten honestly.

12 Variations on a Theme

No pleasure endures, unseasoned by variety

PUBLILIUS SYRUS, FIRST CENTURY BC

In the 40 years since he invented Scrabble, Alfred Butts has played or heard about almost every conceivable variation in the game. Luckily, though, Butts is not one of those egomaniacs who believes what he has created is a masterpiece that cannot be tampered with. Butts, like his successor, Jim Brunot, loves bending the Scrabble rules to suit the playing conditions.

As Butts points out, if you played the game the way he originally conceived it, you would not get a 50-point bonus for using all seven tiles in a single move, the game would not end just because one player used up all his tiles, and the first person out would not receive the end-of-game windfall of double the total of his opponents' remaining tiles.

'There are some people who say you must play by the directions,' he said, 'but I don't believe that.' And Jim Brunot has often said that you should make up your own house rules and play that way.

With that blessing from the game's maker, Scrabble players have come up with such exotic variations as Blank or Ecology Scrabble, Double Bag Scrabble, Anagram Scrabble, Stopwatch Scrabble, and even Scrabble-in-reverse: a diabolical game called Unscrabble.

The following, then, are some tried and tested variations on the game of Scrabble with which you might like to experiment. Before you start, you should remember two things: first, always spell out house rules clearly before a game, to prevent arguments, which can become heated during a match. And second, remember the plea of both Butts and Brunot: 'Look, it's only a game.'

Jacks to open

The orthodox Scrabble start goes as follows: each player draws a tile from the pool and the one nearest to the beginning of the alphabet goes first. All he has to do is use two or more tiles and place one of them on the centre star.

The problem with the standard start is that the first player may decide to open with a word like *xi* or *qua* or some other short word and thereby launch a game so tight that it almost strangles before it gets off the ground.

To make the start more interesting and to let the early game 'breathe', a lot of Scrabble players opt for a compulsory big-word start, which I call 'Jacks to Open', as in Jackpot Poker. Under this variation, the player who draws the tile closest to *A* has the chance to start (and double his opening score), but only if he has a word of five letters or more. If he cannot make a five-letter word, then he must say 'Pass' and relinquish the start to the next competitor. In four-handed Scrabble this goes on until one player can make a five-letter opener.

If nobody can form a five-letter word, then the prerogative passes back to the original opener, who then attempts to make a four-letter word, for which he will still get the double word bonus – as would one of his opponents if he could have made a five-letter word. If Player 1 still cannot make a word four letters in length, he again passes, and so on, with the mandatory word length shrinking until somebody can go. If you cannot open, you must pass, and you may not use that pass to exchange tiles.

Aces to open

The start of 'Aces to Open' is merely a more deadly version of 'Jacks to Open' and involves upping the ante. The player who draws the starting letter closest to *A* can only go if he can make a seven-letter word. If that is not possible, the player must pass and give each opponent a chance for a seven-letter bonus opener. Then, in rotation, each player has an opportunity for a six-letter word to open, then a five-, then a four-, and so forth, until somebody breaks the deadlock. As in 'Jacks to Open', no player can use a passed turn to exchange letters from the tile pool during the prestart manoeuvring.

The auction start

The 'Auction Start' is admittedly gimmicky, but it can be fun in a four-handed social game. The same rules apply, as above, with the players agreeing in advance on the minimum length of the starting word. Suppose they agree on four letters. Probably three of them find they can make a four-letter word. The starter is then determined by each consecutive player calling out the first letter of the word he proposes to put down. If a player wishes to play cagey or cannot make a four-letter word, he may pass. The one with the highest starting letter gets the start and collects the double-word bonus. Incidentally, an alert player might deliberately call low and concede the start if he realizes he can capitalize on a previously announced letter and build a better-scoring word than if he started with a four-letter word of his own.

Blank or Ecology Scrabble

This variation of Scrabble has proved extremely popular because it brightens the game, increases the chance of seven-letter words, and introduces a poker-style constant 'wild card' into play. I call it 'Ecology Scrabble' because it involves recycling the blank.

Standard Scrabble rules apply until a blank appears on the board. Under basic rules the blank tile remains fixed to the board for the remainder of the game and represents whatever letter was designated by the player who placed it. In Blank Scrabble any player can gain possession of the blank, providing it is his turn, by replacing it with a real letter that matches the original designation.

For example, if Player 1 places the word *paste* on the board and uses a blank for the letter *P*, then Player 2 can retrieve the blank by putting a real *P* in its place. The blank is then 'clean' and can be used by Player 2 to represent any letter he chooses in a subsequent word. Switching a letter for a blank can only be done when it is a player's turn and does not constitute a move. Just because a player claims the blank, it does not force him to use it in the next turn, and he may hold it in his rack for as long as he wants before replaying it.

If a player chooses to 'pass' on a turn and discard some of his letters, he is not entitled to claim the blank as part of that turn. In this variation both blanks can be used at least half a dozen times, and there is still room for strategy. Late in a game, a player can freeze the blank by playing it and calling it some letter for which all tiles are already exposed on the board. For instance, the player who used the blank in the word *paste* could have called the word *haste* and disabled the blank for the remainder of the game if both *H* tiles had been on the board. This strategy of neutering the blank becomes important in the final stages of the game.

Double Bag Scrabble

This is a variation for the people who complain that there are too many vowels in the Scrabble set. In fact, there are 42 vowels and 56 consonants, but that is slight consolation for the player with a rackful of *O*s and *E*s – especially if he does not know such vowel-consuming words as *cooee* and *hoopoe*.

Butts admits that one of the most frequent complaints about the game's structure is that there are too many tiles with the letter *I* on them. Butts said, 'When I invented the game and was working out the tile distribution, I wanted to make sure I could get long words with the letters instead of a lot of little short words. The letter *I* is in there quite a lot because I like the endings you use like *ion* and *ing*. I also like to get words you can add prefixes and often suffixes to.'

However, even Butts and his wife, Nina, it seems have become frustrated by the plethora of vowels in the game. Double Bag Scrabble is a game variation that Butts now plays regularly.

Before the game, you separate the vowels and consonants into two bags. At the start of play you are free to draw as many consonants or vowels as you like up to the regulation seven tiles. After a while, most people average out to four consonants and three vowels. Throughout the game you may restock your rack from either bag, which means that after each turn, you have to make a decision on which way to weigh your hand.

The immediate reaction is to draw more heavily from the consonant bag to increase your chances of snaring high-scoring tiles like the Z and the X. Butts knocks that strategy down: 'Drawing from the consonant bag all the time to get high-count letters won't do you any good unless you draw vowels to go with them. You'll find you have to draw from both bags, and in this variation you never get your hand lopsided.'

One stipulation is that you must draw all your letters at once, such as two tiles from the consonant bag and immediately one from the vowel bag if you need three letters. It is illegal to draw several consonants, look at them, and then head for the vowels.

Double Bag Scrabble has become standard fare in the Butts household, and it was one variation Butts suggested to Jim Brunot for inclusion in the revised rules. 'He didn't do anything with it, but he did send me a supply of those plastic tile bags, and I stuck my own labels on them marked 'vowels' and 'consonants' and gave them to friends.'

Solitaire Scrabble

The game of Scrabble was designed for two, three or four players, although it is best when played by two people. The fact that it is a game that can be played successfully by an odd number of competitors has always been a big selling point.

But a lot of people do not realize that you can also play an interesting game of Scrabble by yourself. I'll admit that when I first heard of Solitaire Scrabble, I was dubious. It seemed to me only human nature that I would cheat, maybe even subconsciously, when playing an imaginary opponent. I've since discovered, though, that Solitaire can be played honestly, and it can be exciting. It's great practice, and there's absolutely no pressure from an opponent on how much time you take per turn – hence more seven-letter words.

There are three variations of Solitaire Scrabble. One method is to play with a single rack of tiles, and instead of the average 15 turns in a game, you get more than 30. You play Standard Scrabble rules, keep restocking your rack, and take turn after turn. You keep a tally of your total game scores and each time try to improve on your best one.

The second method is to play with two racks and play against an imaginary opponent. The third method is to turn all the tiles face up on the table and, armed with a dictionary, deliberately try to build high-scoring words.

The best version, in my opinion, is the second one, played with two racks. To make it even more competitive, I have made the following refinements: After playing from rack 1, I do not immediately replenish it with tiles, but instead turn the depleted rack away from me and pick up rack 2. I then play rack 2 and turn it away without drawing fresh letters. Then I pick up rack 1, and only then do I draw the required letters to bring it back up to seven tiles. After playing rack 1 again, I turn it away, replenish rack 2, and play a word from it. If you delay the restocking process, there is always an element of doubt over what letters will be in the opposing rack when it is time to play again.

I play this variation under basic Scrabble rules and play it as defensively as any normal hand – never setting up triple-word opportunities for the opposing hand. You can get so carried away in this game, looking for seven-letter plays, that you actually forget what letters are lurking in the other rack. And because you are playing yourself, the competition is pretty even, and the scores remain neck and neck.

The third version of playing with all tiles exposed on the table is a good vocabulary builder, but it is not as much fun and nowhere near as satisfying.

Theme Scrabble

Theme Scrabble refers to versions of the game where the only words permitted must pertain to a previously agreed upon theme. For example, if you decide politics is your game theme, then words used must be like *vote*, *elect*, *campaign*, *platform*, *poll* and *candidate*. In these post-Watergate days, presumably, you could also use words like *burgled*, *crook*, *bugging*, *bribe* and, possibly, *expletive deleted*.

You can also play proper name Scrabble in which anything goes, from *Harold Wilson* to *Piccadilly Circus*, from *Polos* to *Mars bars*, from *Jack and Jill* to *Jack the Ripper*.

Sporting Scrabble can be fun, too. For example in Cricket Scrabble the names of Test players are permissible along with such obvious cricketing terms as *six*, *stonewall*, *slips*, *pads*, *stumps*, *bouncer*, *wide* and, possibly, '*howzat*'.

Sexy, Vulgar or Dirty Scrabble can be entertaining, though I won't reproduce a game board here! Usually you are permitted to use any part of the body, all amorous words, and any expression in the vernacular you can get past your opponent.

In Cinema or Hollywood Scrabble you are permitted to use the names of well-known actors, words from popular film titles, plus such cinema terms as *camera*, *dolly*, *zoom*, *flashback* and *Oscar*.

There's also Geography Scrabble in which you can use only names of countries, cities, lakes, rivers and so forth.

Obviously, the rules for Theme Scrabble are loose and consist of what you think is a fair thing at the time. The beauty of it, especially if four people are playing, is that you can take turns thinking up themes: there's Gourmet Scrabble, in which each word has to have something to do with the kitchen, or TV Scrabble, in which every word has to have a link to a TV programme – or be a term used in the industry, such as the words *ratings*, *commercial* or *network*.

Some of the most fun in these theme games is not the actual playing of a theme word but the often tortured reasoning by the player trying to get the word accepted. This applies especially in Story Scrabble, in which each word played must continue on from the last played word to make a sentence.

Stopwatch Scrabble

This is the way the experts play the game. It's a clock-racing game for hot players. It's the way I imagine chess genius Bobby

Fischer would play Scrabble. In this variation, literally every second counts and there is no room for the dodderer or the dawdler.

Scrabble champion Frank Kuehnrich hates to play the game any other way and if you ever get to play at a place like the Chess Center Game House in New York, then this is the version to expect.

Shortly after winning his 1975 New York title against 850 opponents, Kuehnrich said, 'Scrabble against the clock is the only way to play. Like in chess, you are given so many minutes per game to make your moves. It's up to the individual player to decide which moves are worth ten seconds of time and which moves are worth four minutes.'

At the New York Chess Center, each player is permitted 15 minutes per game to make all his moves. He is also given a bonus three minutes to provide time for keeping score. That means each player has 18 minutes to complete his game, and it is up to each player to budget his time clock as he goes along. It averages out at about one minute a turn, there usually being between 15 and 18 moves per player in a two-man game. That doesn't mean, though, that each turn takes a minute. A player may take five minutes on a desperate gamble for a seven-letter play and then sprint through later turns in seconds to balance his time clock.

There are two clocks alongside the board, and players stop and start their opponent's timepieces as in championship chess. The big difference is that in chess you lose if your clock runs out of time. In Chess Center Scrabble you are still in the game if your 18 minutes runs out, but you are penalized 10 points for every minute you go over the limit.

This version of timed Scrabble should not be confused with Tournament Scrabble, in which each player is permitted a flat two (or three) minutes per turn to complete a move. If he fails to place a word in that time, the prerogative passes to his opponent, who also then starts a clock race. In tournament play it makes no difference if you drop one word in 10 seconds and a second word in 45 seconds and then are stumped on a hard one that makes your next two (or three) minutes run out. You can't 'bank' time not used on a short turn.

Kuehnrich thinks this method is a foolish one. 'Their system is wrong. The only way to time Scrabble is the same way as chess is timed. You get a set time for the complete game. Then it is up to you how much time you spend on individual moves. Some moves take seconds and others take minutes. To şet an arbitrary three minutes per move is just wrong. The timing has to be organized so that it is the player's prerogative whether he spends a short time or a long time on a specific move.'

For players who aren't in the 18-minute-a-game league, I suggest a 30-minute time limit. Then as you get better, you and your opponent can trim minutes from the time bank until you are down to the cut-throat level.

Anagram Scrabble

Players who enjoy deciphering anagrams or who like doing newspaper word games will enjoy Anagram Scrabble. Under this variation a player, when his turn comes, is permitted to re-arrange any word on the board providing he meets two conditions. The first is that he adds at least one more letter to the existing word, and the second is that the rearranged letters form an acceptable word and that interlocking words still make sense. The player then receives full credit for any new or altered words, but any previously covered premium letter and premium word squares are disregarded.

On Board 44 the Anagram Scrabbler attacks the word *navel* (*H* 11–15). He decides to rearrange that word and along the way picks up points for several other altered words and one new one.

On Board 45 he has added one letter, an *E*, and rearranged the letters so that they now extend from squares *H*–11 through *H*–15 and spell the word *leaven*. The word *vile* (15 *F–I*) has become *vine*, the word *bent* (11 *F–I*) has become *beet*, and the player has created a new two-letter word *lo* (10 *H–I*). He receives face value scores for all four words.

There is another version of Anagram Scrabble, which is a

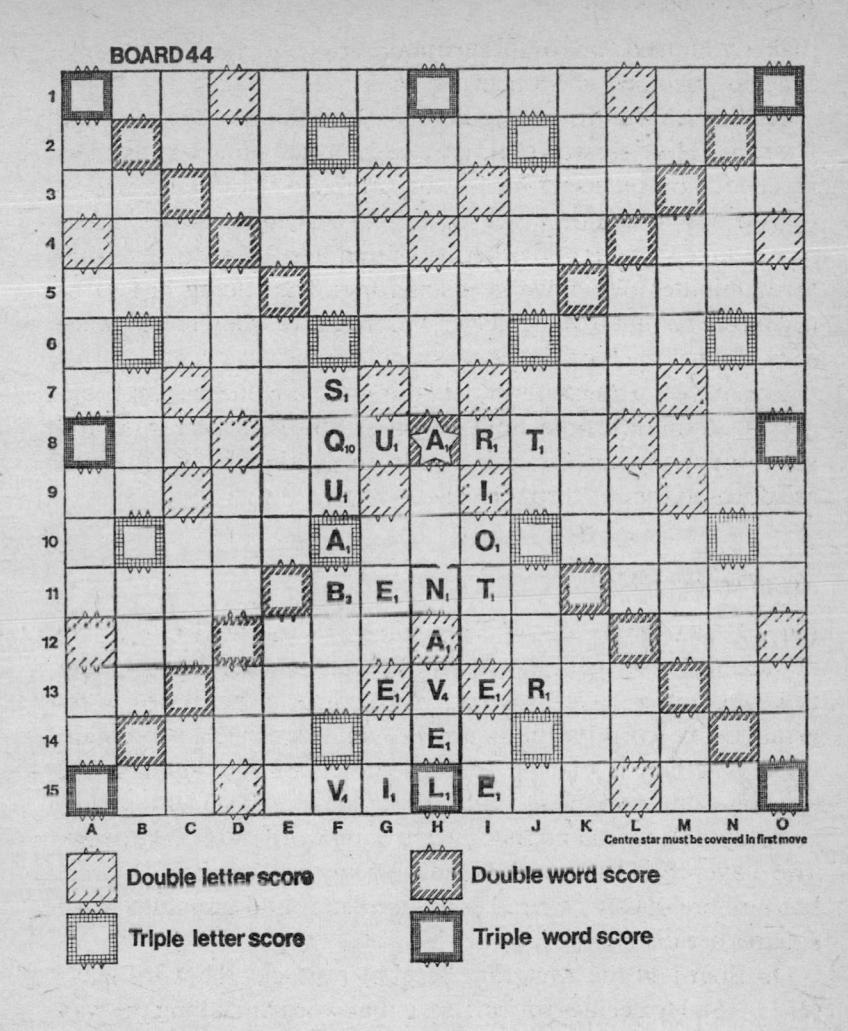

BOARD 44

Centre star must be covered in first move

Double letter score

Double word score

Triple letter score

Triple word score

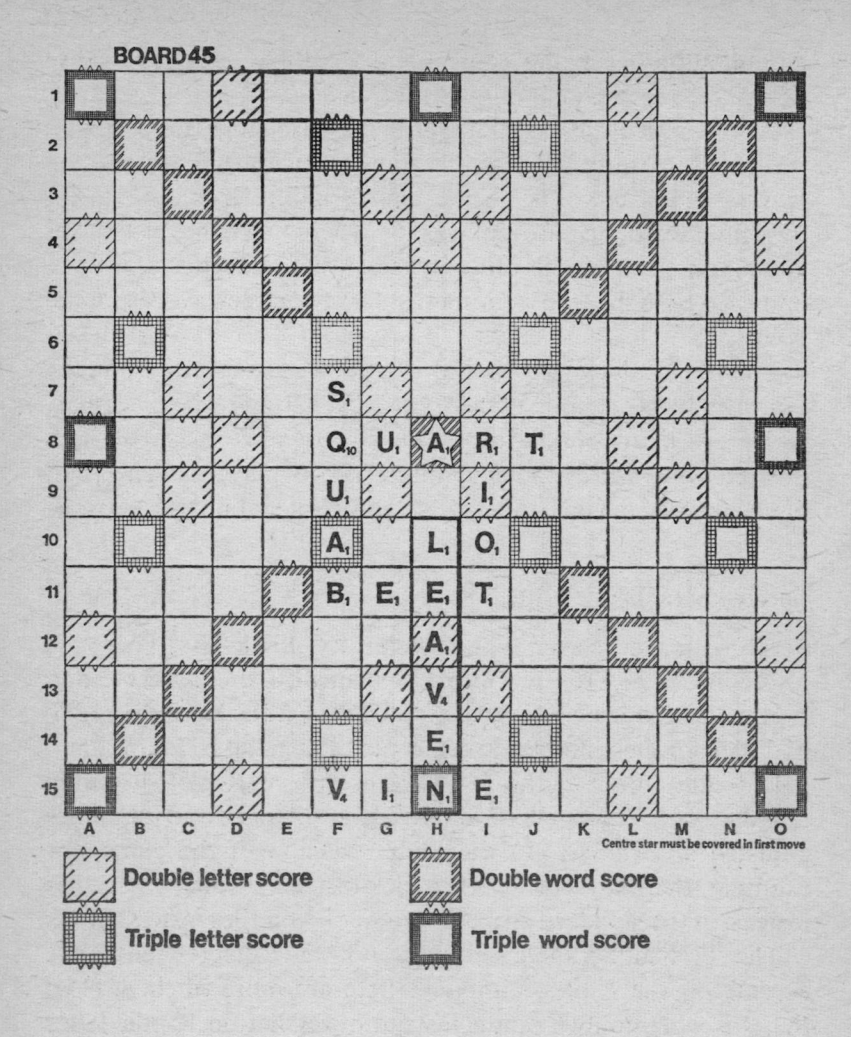

BOARD 45

Centre star must be covered in first move

Double letter score   Double word score

Triple letter score   Triple word score

combination of Anagram and Blank Scrabble. It is designed to permit the repeated use of high-scoring letters.

At the start of his turn, a player may exchange any letter on the board for any letter in his hand, providing the transition leaves complete words on the board. Before laying down his own final word, he may make as many letter switches as he likes in a single turn, but he can only substitute one letter at a time, and each time the transaction must leave complete words on the board.

The player does not receive any points for these exchanges, but does have the advantage of gaining access to better letters, which are then counted in the usual way when he finally lays down his own word. By using this variation, players can get their hands on the big guns, the Z, Q, X and J, several times in a game.

Foreign Scrabble

Scrabble can be played with Russian Cyrillic letters. There are also editions in French, German, Spanish, Dutch, Arabic and Afrikaans. Some people have even extracted the letters K, Y, W and Z from their standard sets to play the game in Latin. Playing foreign Scrabble, though, is not just a matter of switching languages – letter distributions have to be changed and tile values adjusted accordingly. In the Dutch version of the game, for example, there are two letter J tiles instead of one, 10 N tiles instead of the standard six, and a total of 18 E tiles instead of 12.

The French Scrabble set does not have acute and grave accents on the E tiles, although there are more of them (15); the Q is worth only 8 points instead of regulation 10; the letter M is worth only 2 points instead of 3; and five letters – W, X, Y, Z and K – are all worth 10 points each.

There is no Y in the German language, but there is a Y tile in German Scrabble. It makes German players adept at such foreign words as *yacht* and *yak*.

Foreign Scrabble is a great variation of the game if you are trying to learn a new language. Even if your vocabulary in that language is limited to three- and four-letter words, it is fun; and, more important for the language student, it forces you to think in the foreign language. It's no good thinking in English of the word *door*, for example, and then trying to translate it as *porte* in French.

Unscrabble

Fittingly, the last Scrabble variation is Scrabble in reverse, a game called 'Unscrabble'.

Unscrabble is a perfect climax for one of those times when your board is crammed with brilliant words at the end of a normal game and you are reluctant to demolish it.

Unscrabble does ultimately clear the board, but does it with the finesse of a dainty eater. The procedure goes like this. The winner of the regular game removes at least one, but not more than six, tiles from the board. The tiles he lifts must all come from a single word on the board, and the letters he leaves behind must form complete words that, Scrabble style, properly connect with other words and lead back to the centre star. Then the opponent plays. The game of Unscrabble ends when all the tiles have been removed from the board or a stalemate has developed where no more tiles can be removed without leaving incomplete words on the grid.

The game can be varied by changing the maximum number of removable letters in each turn. One way to do that is to roll dice, with each player being required to pick up the number of tiles shown on the dice roll.

There are two scoring systems for Unscrabble. The simplest is that each player receives face value for any letter he removes. The score can be added as you go along, or you can pile your plunder in front of you and total it up at the end. The second, more intricate scoring is to pay full value for premium letter and premium word squares. The bonuses are awarded to the player who uncovers the square concerned. As in real Scrabble, the bonuses can only be claimed once.

PART 4
VOCABULARY

13 The Great Dictionary Dispute

'twas brillig, and the slithy toves
did gyre and gymble in the wabe:
all mimsy were the borogroves,
and the mome raths outgrabe
LEWIS CARROLL, *Through the Looking Glass*

Carroll's warning to 'beware the Jabberwock, my son', holds special meaning for the Scrabble player because this is one field in which Jabberwocks thrive. A cunning Jabberwock, with all his meaningless nonsense words, can hide all night behind the Tumtum tree.

One of the most difficult judgments in the game is to know when your opponent is indulging in Jabberwockery or when he actually has a legitimate word that only sounds like something out of Alice's Wonderland. For example, *bandersnatch* is Jabberwockery, but *bandicoot* is not.

Carroll's protagonist killed the Jabberwock with his 'vorpal sword'. Unfortunately, the only way a Scrabble player can dispatch his is to outgun him with his dictionary.

There are roughly 500,000 words in a normal unabridged English dictionary, and a reasonable vocabulary is 50,000 to 60,000 words. Our brains actually have the capacity to store all those half a million words plus every word in French, German, Chinese and Swahili, but unfortunately most of us utilize only a fraction of our potential.

When it comes to Scrabble, a player with 75,000 words in his memory bank is going to start a game with an advantage over the player who has a mere 50,000. This does not mean, though, that the walking dictionary automatically is going to win – I've seen players with wide vocabularies beaten time and again by more limited opponents, who compensate with a flair for unscrambling anagrams and with a knack for tile placement.

The obvious solution is to build your word knowledge. Read a dictionary every day. That's what former American vice-president Spiro Agnew used to do. How else do you think he could come up with such expressions as 'nattering nabobs of negativism'?

Just think of it: If you read, understood, and committed to memory 10 words a day, you would have 70 fresh words in your repertoire at the end of the first week and more than 3,600 new words hoarded away by the end of the year. And if, to start, you concentrated on good Scrabble words – the tricky, two-, three- and four-letter ones containing high-scoring letters – then pretty soon your word arsenal would be heavily and impressively stocked.

This section contains tips on useful Scrabble words plus a few pointers on how to extend a reasonable word on the board into a better word and a run-down on those lucrative nuggets, the seven-letter words. It also has a few words of warning about dictionary inconsistencies that can cost you a game unless you are fully aware of which dictionary is considered kosher in the house where the contest is being played.

For example, the word *ja* is banned by the Concise Oxford, but is permitted if you are playing with Funk & Wagnalls, where it is listed as an interjection and an adverb meaning 'yes' in German. Funk & Wagnalls is the official arbiter in tournament play across the United States, so *ja* is an important, strategic two-letter word. In several other major American dictionaries, however, including the unabridged Random House, it is listed as foreign, and therefore banned. In the Concise Oxford, as I mentioned, it is not listed at all and in the complete Oxford it appears only as an obsolete variant of the word *jay*. In Webster's (unabridged) it is not listed except as an abbreviation of 'joint account'.

Here is another two-letter discrepancy. The word *te* is in the

Oxford and is also acceptable in Random House as a variant of the musical note *ti*, but it is not permitted if you play by Funk & Wagnalls.

Ironically, you are not even safe if you get hold of one of those Scrabble word guides, like the 'authorized list' first published by Jacob Orleans and Edmund Jacobson back in 1953 when Scrabble was a new craze. If you try to play the word *zax* and then, when challenged, claim it appears three times in the word guide, you'd be right, whether you were using the American or British version. But if you check the purported source of the original New York edition of the word guide, the Funk & Wagnalls, you'll find they've axed the *zax*. The Oxford gives *zax* as an accepted version of *sax*, and it still appears in Webster's and Random House as *zax*, a tool for trimming roofing slates, but in Funk & Wagnalls it is spelled only as *sax*.

Scrabble's longtime producer and marketer in America, Jim Brunot, told me that dictionary squabbling was one thing he never dreamed of as an offshoot of the game. One thing that bugged him, especially, was the way the original rules were worded concerning foreign words.

'We said that any words were permitted if they were found in a standard dictionary except capitalized words and words designated as foreign words, then abbreviations, etc.,' Brunot said. 'We had more trouble with the "designated foreign word" rule than anything else, I think. I wish we hadn't made that reference that way. The dictionary I always played with back then used those two little parallel marks to distinctly stamp a word as foreign. There was no argument. Unfortunately, it differs so much now between dictionaries. Somebody, for example, plays the word for 'yes' in German, *ja*, and it's in the dictionary. Then somebody else says, "Well, why can't I have *oui* for 'yes' in French?" Or Spanish for "maybe". It's a very frequent source of conflict.' (Actually, *oui* is permissible as an adverb for 'yes' in French in Funk & Wagnalls, and so is *si*, meaning 'yes' in Portuguese, Italian and Spanish. *Oui* is banned in all Oxford dictionaries but the word *si* is listed as a musical note in the full Oxford.)

This is one of the reasons why Brunot claims to be more embarrassed than flattered when he meets people at cocktail parties and is introduced as 'Mr Scrabble'. 'People are always wanting to pick arguments about "Is such and such a word?" It's almost unbelievable sometimes. We've had telephone calls from all over the States, from California, everywhere. They've come at all hours from people wanting me to be arbiter on a challenged game.'

Brunot always resisted the idea of having a standard dictionary as the Scrabble Bible, but on reflection said, 'I suppose with a tournament you have to have one.' He had need of one himself in a game several days before we talked at his winter retreat on Hilton Head Island in South Carolina.

'I was playing a friend,' he recalled, 'and she played the word *booted*. It was in a good position for me; so I played *unbooted* to extend it up to catch a triple-word square. She challenged me, and I knew I'd won, but unfortunately the dictionary I have here doesn't contain the word *unbooted*.'

Despite his reputation for being a passive, gentlemanly Scrabble player, Jim Brunot is stubborn when he thinks he has been robbed. 'I kept looking for that word,' he said, 'and I found it too. It was in the Oxford Dictionary, down at the local library. By then it was too late, of course. I'd been booted.'

Which brings up the point of how does a word get into the dictionary in the first place?

Each time there is a major revision of a dictionary, the editors seek out new words and, often, new meanings for old words. New words come into use every day. Some are cult words that are coined to fit a political or social situation and then fade into oblivion. Some remain as part of the language even though their meaning may change drastically over the years.

The space race brought a welter of new words like *re-entry*, *module*, *nose cone* and *retro-rocket*. It also brought new meanings for old words like NASA's use of the word *nominal* to mean

'Everything is going fine' and *anomalous* when things are going disastrously.

The civil rights movement of the late 1950s and early 1960s brought the words *desegregation* and *sit-in* and gave the word *demonstration* an additional definition as a parade of protesters. The Vietnam War brought the overworked words *escalation* and *defoliation* and *pre-emptive* as in 'pre-emptive reaction strike'. In politics came the words *détente*, *co-existence* and *summitry*.

In the recent vernacular the word *ball* came to mean 'to have sexual intercourse', not 'a dance', and, in reverse, the evolution of the word *jazz* changed it from a black American expression meaning 'to have intercourse' into a type of music. It's not that long ago that words like *transistorize* and *vaccinate* and *recyclable* and *introvert* and *overkill* and *biodegradable* were not in existence. And nobody knows how long *gay* will be accepted as meaning 'homosexual' or if *swinger* will for ever more be regarded as a definition of a person who engages in group sex.

Sidney Landau, formerly editor-in-chief at Funk & Wagnalls and currently editor-in-chief for a new Doubleday dictionary, said, 'Until we have good grounds for believing that a particular term will remain in use for a number of years, we must postpone including it in the dictionary.' He also said that all slang expressions, except the most common, were usually excluded from general dictionaries and so were the 'most vulgar and taboo' expressions. Landau said, 'Dictionaries thus tend, however unintentionally, to act as a conservative influence on the language as a whole.'

Once a word is selected for inclusion in the dictionary, it is then worked over by the dictionary staff, who will write the definition or definitions, and by the publishing house's panel of professors and English scholars. They check etymologies, the classification of terms (for example, vulgar, archaic, and so forth), pronunciations and synonyms. Only then is the word ready for inclusion in the next revised edition of the big book.

To some people, a dictionary is a dictionary is a dictionary. As long as it is thick enough, it is bound to have nearly all the same words as a competitor. It may come as a surprise to people, but each dictionary does have its own style and flavour – even though lexicographers claim they strive to make the words used in describing each entry as explicit and as colourless as possible to avoid misinterpretation.

The differences between English English, American English, Australian English, Scottish English and so on are far greater than matters of spelling and pronunciation; whole chunks of vocabulary are particular to each. And dictionary-makers vary widely in their acceptance of new terms, obsolete terms, slang, dialect and cultural variations. Perhaps the dictionary to run to if all else fails is Webster's, but it's a trifle heavy to pass around a Scrabble table.

I hope you can see after all this that a Scrabble house without a dictionary is a breeding ground for Jabberwocks. In fact, playing without a dictionary at hand can really put the 'kaibosh' on a game.

And look *that* up in your Concise Oxford!

14 Two-letter Words

When I play Scrabble with the game's mentor, Alfred Butts, I get the impression that the original version of the game was meant for more genteel times. He permits the use of a dictionary to check spelling, 'as long as you don't browse through it looking for words,' and he doesn't like the tactic of using two-letter words as defensive strategy to keep the board tight. 'I like to play an open game . . . to give everybody a chance to get their words down,' he said.

Consequently, Butts does not place as much importance on the knowledge of two-letter words as tournament players do. For example, he did not know that the words *ma* and *pa* were acceptable. 'We'd never accept those,' he said.

Despite Mr Butts's sentiments, it is imperative that you recognize some of the odd two-letter words (including the word *od*) that are legal and can act as good hook-words for high-scoring seven-letter words. If ever you doubt the value of a two-letter word, remember the point made earlier in the book on how to use the single letter *X* to score 48 points.

According to most unabridged dictionaries, there are between 60 and 70 permissible two-letter words. Some good players know them all, and it is advisable to commit as many to memory as possible. If you can't memorize at least half of them, then at least scan the following list occasionally, and maybe a strange one, like *ex* or *xi*, will stick in your mind and surface as a winning play in a later game.

Another thing is that a player who knows a lot of these can often hoodwink a player who doesn't. After all, if you have been burned by challenging the word *em*, which is a word, you might be reluctant to challenge *ed*, which is not.

These, then, are the most accepted two-letter words:
ad ah ai am an as at ax aw ay be by do eh el em en er ex fa go
ha he hi ho id if in is it jo la li lo ma me mi mu my na no nu
od of oh on or ow ox pa pi re so ti to up us we xi ye.

Those words are all acceptable if you're playing with the Concise Oxford dictionary. If you are playing with the complete Oxford, all 13 volumes of it (or the micro-film version which I have), then you can also use the words *ae, ar, de, os, si, ut* and *wo*.

If you're feeling totally magnanimous and accept obsolete words from the big Oxford, your board could also feature such two-letter offerings as *aa, ba, el, ja, ka* and *pe*.

I have listed all variations because two-letter words are of critical importance in Scrabble. In future word lists, though, I have restricted permissible words to those found in the Concise Oxford.

One trap not to get into when playing two-letter words is to watch an opponent play the word *en* or *em* and then blithely assume that all letters in the alphabet can be used in that fashion. Not so. The words *en* and *em* do stand for those letters in the alphabet, but they also stand for printers' measures. Most letters of the alphabet, in fact, take phonetic three-letter spellings and are listed separately in the dictionary under *bee, cee, dee, eff, gee, jay, kay, ell* (also *el*), *pee, are* (also *ar*), *ess, tee, vee* and *ex*. The vowels and the *Y* are spelled as they look, and so are the *Q* (also *cue*) and the *W*, surprisingly enough, although the *W* can also be spelled *doubleyou*. The letter *H* forms a good word, *aitch*, and so does the *Z*, which can be spelled either as *zed* or with the American-English spelling and pronunciation *zee*.

Once you have memorized these, you have a great source of short words for plurals. For example, the plural of the letter *Q*, as in 'Mind your *p*'s and *q*'s', can be spelled with the apostrophe or simply as *q*s, according to some major dictionaries.

That ploy is not listed in the preceding list of two-letter words because the whole idea of using letters of the alphabet is often disputed, let alone pluralizing them. The British Scrabble Championship rules ban all letter sounds, while American and Australian tournament rules do not allow you to use *q*s or *w*s or *c*s as the plurals of letters of the alphabet. Some house rules, too, have a blanket ban on letters of the alphabet – whether they be *q*s, *aitches* or *betas*.

If you want to play strictly by the book, though, some dictionaries do list '*qs* – plural of *q*' as well as '*ws*' as plural of *w* and '*ys*' as a version of the plural of the letter *y*. The *y* plural can also be spelled *wyes*. The plural for the letter *o* appears as *os* or *oes* – take your pick – and *x* becomes *exes*. In the case of the letter *z*, I can literally say it is last but not least. The last letter in the alphabet has four plural variations. They are *z*'s, *zs*, *zeds* and *zees*.

This whole argument, though, is one that must be settled amicably, I hope, in individual households.

15 Three-letter Words

Once you have etched the two-letter tricksters in your mind, it is time to tackle the three-letter words. And what better, or more orderly, place to start than with three-letter words, which can be made by adding a single letter to a two-letter word already on the board?

A large repertoire of these words is a great Scrabble asset – especially when you are angling for the 50-point bonus that a seven-letter word brings. The reason is simple. Often opponents won't leave an easy opening for a seven-letter play. They'll deliberately shut off an exposed *S* or an exposed *D* or *T*. Yet they will blindly leave the word *ha* exposed for you, and you can tag a *P* on to it to make the three-letter word *hap* going horizontally and a seven-letter word like *persona* going vertically.

Some of these two-into-three words are obvious – words like *at* or *in* being transformed into *bat*, *cat*, *fat*, *hat*, or *bin*, *tin*, *kin* or *win* by merely adding a letter in front. And by placing a letter on the tail, words like *ho* or *jo* can easily be extended into *hob*, *hop*, *hog* and *hod* or *jog*, *job* or *jot*. The ones to remember, though, are the obscure ones – like putting an *M* after the word *is* to make *ism* or a *Z* in front of *ax* to make *zax*.

The following are a few unusual three-letter words that can be formed by adding a single letter to an acceptable two-letter word already on the board. The new letter is added in front in some words and at the rear on others.

Add an A:
aby ado ago aha ait ana are aye era yea

Add a B:
bah bay ben bow bye gob job lab lob nob nub orb web

Add a C:
cam can caw cay cod cow cox hic lac mac orc tic

Add a D:
aid dan dor dup hod odd pad sod tod wed

Add an E:
axe aye bee eel ego hie hoe ide ore pie wee

Add an F:
fad fah fan fay fen fid fox off ref

Add a G:
erg gad gat gel gem gin hag jog mag mug nog tig

Add an H:
fah hex hid hod how lah noh pah soh

Add an I:
ire

Add a J:
jam jaw jay jot jow

Add a K:
erk kay ken kid kit

Add an L:
awl bel ell lah lam lax lay lit low lox mil owl til

Add an M:
aim ism lam mad mas maw may mho mid mow mum rem

Add an N:
awn ben ern fan nit noh nor own wen yon

Add an O:
goo loo oho oof ooh too

Add a P:
dop hap pah pap pas paw pax phi pox yep

Add a Q:
nil

Add an R:
dor err far lar mir nor rad rem tor

Add an S:
ais ays has jos las mas pas sad sax sex sin sis soh

Add a T:
ait het ort tam tan tit tod tor tup

Add a U:
emu sou

Add a V:
lav rev van vas vat vex vow

Add a W:
haw how jaw maw mew wad wax way wen wis yew

Add an X:
lax lox mix pax pix pox six

Add a Y:
bey hey hoy kay may soy yah yam yen yin yod yon

Add a Z:
adz zax

Once you get into the thought channel of automatically seeing word extensions, even by one letter in either direction, it's not long before you start exploiting two-letter words by extending them from both ends in a single turn. Then you can seize on an exposed *ai* and jump on both ends with your seven tiles to make a word like *m-ai-lboxes* for a bonus. Or *j-od-hpur*, which wouldn't be a bonus, but would still give you a healthy score.

Three-letter words that don't originate from two-letter ones are also of prime importance in Scrabble – especially the ones with high-scoring consonants like *fez* and *qua* and *pyx*. The following is a list of some good ones, not all of them by any means:

aga alp auk ave bot bur cob cog cos coz cud dak dap daw dub
eau edh eff eft eta eth feu fey fez fob gee gey gib gig gyp jew
kea kef kip lea lug lux moa mob nix nth ova pyx qua raj sac sal
tun tut ugh vee veg vet via voe wag war wiz woo you yap
zag zed zee zip zoo

16 Four-, Five- and Six-letter Words

It is conceivable, though I've never seen anyone do it, for a player to complete a 15-letter word on a single play. In theory, a player could thread his seven letters through a patchwork of letters already on the board and wind up with a 15-letter epic like *equiponderating* (the art of counterbalancing). For argument's sake, assume that the bottom row on the board reads – – – – – *ON – – RATING*, and this lucky hypothetical player happens to have the letters *P D Q U E I E* on his rack and the word *equiponderating* in his head.

I mention this remote possibility to illustrate the endless combinations imaginable in Scrabble and to explain why, in this chapter, I make no attempt to list all four-, five- and six-letter words available. For that, you would have to staple a dictionary on the back of this book.

Instead, I have concentrated on the big four – the *Z*, *Q*, *X* and *J*. They are the most profitable tiles because they have the highest point value and are the hardest to place. There is only one of each in the 100 tiles, and unless you are playing Blank or Ecology Scrabble, where letters are recycled, they come round only once in a game.

Although the number of words with a *Z* or a *Q* in them is limited, such words are not *that* scarce, and no player should shy away from them. In fact, once you have memorized a few words like *zloty* and *quetzal* and *phlox* and *jonquil*, you relish the times when your groping fingers pull one of this quartet from the tile pool.

The following word lists contain some of the more rewarding, unusual words using the big four.

Some of the words listed use the main letter more than once, like *hajj* or *huzza*, which would eliminate them unless a player has a blank as well. The list is by no means complete, and all obvious words like *daze*, *doze*, *freeze* or *breeze* have been omitted. Only where a word has a tricky alternative spelling is it included.

Four-letter words with a Z:

adze czar dozy fuze fuzz hazy jazz mazy oozy oyez tzar whiz zebu zein zeta zinc zink zoic zone zoom zori

Four-letter words with a Q:

cinq quad quag quay quid quiz quod

Four-letter words with an X:

apex axis axle axon calx coxa doxy flax flux ibex ilex ixia jinx luxe lynx minx moxa oryx oxer pixy sext taxi

Four-letter words with a J:

hadj hajj jamb jape jarl jazz jell jess jink jinn jinx joey joke jowl judo jute puja raja

Five-letter words with a Z:

azoic azure bezel bonze braze colza cozen dozen diazo fizzy frizz furze furzy fuzee fuzzy gauzy hazel huzza huzzy izzat jazzy kazoo lazar mazer mizen muzzy ouzel ozone pizza razee sizar spitz tazza topaz vizor wizen zambo zebec zibet zinck zloty zombi zonal zooid zoril

Five-letter words with a Q:

pique quaff quail qualm quart quash quean quern queue quill quilt quint quipu quire quirt quoin quoit quoth roque squab toque tuque

Five-letter words with an X :

addax admix affix annex ataxy axial axiom axled beaux borax
buxom calix calyx codex coxae excel exult helix hexad hyrax
infix latex laxly maxim mixen moxie murex nixie oxide oxter
phlox pixie pulex pyxis radix remex taxon toxic unsex varix
xebec xenon

Five-letter words with a J :

fjord hadji hadjj jabot jager jaggy jalap jaspe jazzy jehad
jemmy jenny jerry jihad jimmy jingo jorum joule julep jumbo
junco junta jural jurat rajah thuja

Six-letter words with a Z :

ablaze assize azalea bazaar benzol bezant bezoar blazon blazer
blowzy bonzer borzoi bronzy chintz coryza eczema evzone
fizgig foozle frazil frieze frowzy gazebo guzzle izzard mazuma
mizzen mizzly muzhik ozonic panzer piazza pizzle podzol
razzia razzle seizin sleazy stanza syzygy teazel teazle vizard
vizier vizsla weazen wheeze zaffer zaffre zarape zareba zariba
zebeck zenana zephyr zibeth zigzag zincky zinnia zircon zither
zodiac zombie zonary zonate zooave zounds zygoma zygote
zymase

Six-letter words with a Q :

barque basque bisque caique cinque cirque claque clique cliquy
masque mosque oblique piquet pulque quaere quagga quaggy
quahog quanta quarte quarto quartz quasar quatre quince
quinol quinsy quinta quistle quitch risque roquet sacque
squail squama squill squint toques torque

Six-letter words with an X :

adieux admixt afflux ataxia ataxic axilla coaxes coccyx commix
cortex cruxes dexter duplex efflux elixir exsert extant fixate
fixity flaxen flexor galaxy hallux hexane hexode hexose larynx
luxate matrix meninx oxalic pickax plexor plexus pollex praxis
prolix reflux scolex sextan sexton sixain spadix storax syntax
syrinx thorax vertex vortex xoanon xylene xystus

Six-letter words with a J:

abjure adjure donjon hejira jabber jacana jackal jaeger jalopy jargon jarrah jasmin jasper jejune jennet jerbil jerboa jerkin jetsam jetton jinnee jitney jocose jocund jounce jujube jungly moujik sejant swaraj

17 Seven-letter Bonus Words

When Jim Brunot took over Alfred Butts's game and changed its name from Criss-crosswords to Scrabble, he changed very little else. He did have one innovation, however, that drastically altered the scoring system for the game and also totally changed some competitors' style of play.

Brunot decreed that if you successfully laid down all seven letters in your rack in a single turn, you were entitled to a bonus of 50 points on top of the points you would normally score for that play. Such a move, often a game-winning one, has been called a lot of different things, not all of them flattering, over the years. Brunot called it a 'fifty-point premium word'. I have alternately referred to it as a 'seven-letter play', a 'boardbuster', a 'sweep' or a 'slam'. For a while I considered calling it a 'brunot' in honour of the man who invented the bonus. The American Tournament Scrabble people call it a 'bingo' – an expression loathed by the game's inventor, Butts, because it sounds as if it has been stolen from a certain other board game. But it has been through Tournament Scrabble that the seven-letter play has been perfected. So 'bingo' is spreading. It has not yet reached England, however, where Scrabblers may laconically refer to it as 'hitting the jackpot'.

The bonus play, how and when to make it, is detailed with all its heroics and heartbreaks in the strategy part of the book. What follows here is a list of key word endings, common prefixes, seven-letter words containing the 'big four' letters, and a rundown on the 'satire syndrome' – a tricky code to smoke well-hidden bonus words out of your rack.

To start, the most common source of seven-letter words is to be found in the following word endings: *-ies*, *-ing*, *-ent*, *-ble*, *-iest*,

-ed, -ter. Other endings that give you a good leg up towards a bonus are *-ion, -tion, -tian, -cing, -able, -ment*.

The endings *er* and *est* are the most commonly used in the English language for comparatives and superlatives. For example: *cold, colder, coldest*. This form of word ending is so common that most general dictionaries do not even include it. If a listed word has a normal declension, then *er* and *est* are taken for granted as the comparative and superlative forms. If the word ending is unusual – like *happy, happier, happiest* – then it will be specifically noted. And it will also be listed if the word changes completely, like *bad, worse, worst*.

A good Scrabble player also knows common prefixes like *un-, re-, mis-, inter-*, and so on.

Some letters combine easily with each other to make seven-letter words, whereas others are as compatible as oil and water. That is where the 'satire syndrome' comes in. A few years ago somebody came across the fact that the six-letter word *satire* is one of the most promiscuous words in the language it will mate with practically any other letter to form a seven-letter word. As a matter of fact, as noted earlier, if you add any one of 16 of the 26 letters in the alphabet to the letters in the word *satire* you'll get a bonus word. At tournaments across the United States players use the *satire* test, along with several others like *retina* and *santer*.

Sometimes, though, slavish devotion to these key combinations, coupled with a faulty memory, can bring on an acute attack of nail-biting. In one dismal game, in which I was soundly thrashed, I suddenly found the magic letters *S A T I R E* hidden in my jumbled rack. The seventh letter was an *O*. I ran my time out in a futile letter-shuffling attempt to find the elusive word. Later I checked and found that the letter *O* is one of the ten letters that does not combine with *satire* to make a seven-letter word.

Using *satire* as a building block, you can make a fistful of bonus words by the addition of a single letter. Here are 43 of them:

A – nil
B – baiters
C – raciest, stearic
D – tirades, staider, astride, disrate
E – seriate
F – fairest
G – stagier, gaiters, seagirt, aigrets
H – hastier
I – airiest
J – nil
K – nil
L – retails, realist, saltire, saltier
M – misrate
N – retains, stainer, nastier, retinas, stearin, restain
O – nil
P – parties, traipse, pastier, pirates, piaster, piastre
Q – nil
R – tarries, tarsier
S – satires
T – ratites, tastier, artiste, striate, attires
U – nil
V – nil
W – wariest, waiters, waister
X – nil
Y – nil
Z – nil

The stock letters forming the word *retina* can be teamed with 16 other letters to make a word; in this case, at least 39 of them:

A – nil
B – nil
C – certain
D – detrain, trained
E – trainee, retinae
F – fainter
G – ingrate, granite, tangier, tearing
H – nil

I – inertia
J – nil
K – keratin
L – latrine, retinal, reliant, trenail, ratline
M – raiment, minaret
N – entrain
O – nil
P – pertain, painter, repaint
Q – nil
R – trainer, retrain, terrain
S – stainer, nastier, retinas, retains, stearin
T   nitrate, tertian, nattier, tainter
U – ruinate, urinate, taurine
V – nil
W – tawnier
X – nil
Y – nil
Z – nil

Under the same system, the word *santer* (although unacceptable standing alone) combines with 17 letters for 40 bonus words:

A – nil
B – banters
C – trances, canters, nectars, recants
D – stander
E – earnest, nearest, eastern
F – nil
G – strange, garnets, argents
H – thenars, anthers
I   nastier, retains, stainer, retinas, stearin
J – nil
K – tankers, rankest
L – antlers, saltern
M – smarten, martens
N – tanners
O – treason, senator, roanest, atoners
P – parents, trepans, pastern

Q – nil
R – ranters
S – nil
T – natters
U – saunter, natures
V – taverns, versant, servant
W – nil
X – nil
Y - nil
Z – nil

With words like *trepans*, *stearin* and *striate*, you may think that you'll never shake a seven-letter word from your hand.

However, if you are not yet totally discouraged, then the following list of other seven-letter combinations might be of interest. As in the chapters on useful three-, four-, five- and six-letter words, the list is restricted to unusual words, utilizing the *Z*, *Q*, *X* and *J*.

Seven-letter words with a Z:

apprize azimuth azygous bazooka benzene benzine benzoic benzole bezique britzka buzzard chintzy cognize cozener crozier czardom czarina czarism diarize dozenth elegize emblaze frizzle frizzly fuzzily gizzard lazaret matzoth mazurka mestizo mezuzah muezzin obelize oxidize ozonize quetzal rhizoid rhizome scherzo squeeze swizzle tweezer tzarina zebrine zedoary zeolite zetetic zincify zincing zincked zinkify zinking zooidal zoology zygosis zymosis zymotic zymurgy

Seven-letter words with a Q:

aliquot aquaria aquatic aqueous briquet cacique cliquey coequal coquina coquito cumquat equable equerry jonquil kumquat lacquer liquefy marquee marquis masquer obloquy obsequy parquet picquet piquant quadrat quadric quaffer quahaug quantic quantum quartan quartic quassia querist quetzel quietus quillet quilter quinary quinate quinine quintal quintan

quondam racquet relique requiem rorqual sequela sequent
sequoia siliqua silique squabby squacco squalid squally
squamae squatty squinch squirmy

Seven-letter words with an X:

anthrax aptyrex axillae axolotl biaxial boxcalf bureaux
cachexy calyxes coaxial conflux coxcomb dextral dextran
dextrin dioxide expiate expunge exscind flexile flexion flexure
fluxion foxhole foxtail foxtrot hexagon lexical lexicon maxilla
maximal maxwell mixible noxious overtax oxalate oxidise
oxidize oxytone phalanx pickaxe pyrexia pyrexic saxhorn
saxtuba sextain sextant taxiing tectrix textual toxemia toxemic
triplex xanthic xiphoid

Seven-letter words with a J:

abjurer adjudge adjunct adjurer basenji conjoin jackdaw
jacinth jackpot jaconet jadeite jaggery jargoon jasmine jejunum
jellaba jobbery joinder jollity jonquil jugular jumbuck juniper
juryman jussive sapajou subject subjoin

18 The Word Dump

You don't have to know that *cooee* was originally 'an Australian bushman's shout to attract somebody's attention' or that a *hoopoe* is 'a dazzlingly-plumed European bird'. But if you want to be a good Scrabble player, you *do* have to know that *cooee* and *hoopoe* are indeed legitimate words and are an essential part of Scrabble vocabulary.

Such vowel-crammed words are known as 'dumpers' in the Scrabble business. They are words you pull out of your stockpile when your rack is vowel-heavy and when you don't want to miss a turn by passing in order to get rid of the often duplicated, offending tiles. After all, unless you know about that hoopoe bird, you could be in trouble with a rack of tiles containing the letters $P H O O O E$.

In the strategy part of the book, I discussed rack balancing and the tactic of 'dumping'. Here, then, are a few good dumpers to help you play your way out of trouble rather than forfeit a turn by passing.

adieu aerie aoudad apogee audio aural aureole auricle aurora baboo balata beau bureau cilia cilium cooee cooer eerie eerily emetic epee epopee etui eyrie fiancee guaiac heroic hoodoo hoopoe idiom iguana ileum iliac ionic iota luau melee miaow oleic oolite oolong oribi oriel oriole ovolo paleae peewit piano queue quaere radii radio ratio roue taboo tiara unau voodoo

19 Switch-hitters

Scrabble is a game in which the old adage about 'a bird in the hand' is not necessarily true. A bird in the hand, or should I say a word in the hand, is not always worth two in the bush.

The problem for some players is to shake the branches hard enough to dislodge the other hidden words - words that use identical letters to the one originally chosen but which can be worth more points. For example, I have the seven-letter word *reverse* in my hand. I'm so elated at getting a 50-point bonus that I look no further. But the letters that comprise the word *reverse* also make up the word *reserve*, and there is a chance that by going for the second option, the letter *V* may land on a triple-letter score for 12 points instead of the *S*, which would only be worth 3 points. You may think that the difference of 9 points is miniscule when compared to the 60-plus points you score for the whole move. Just remember it, though, when you lose a game by 8 points. That word *reverse*, incidentally, also makes the word *severer*.

Switch-words give you more freedom when you are looking for spots on the board to attach your words, and often a variation is worth more points. You have the word *faster* in your hand and think how great it would be if it ended in an *E* because you have spotted a prime square to extend a previously played word with an *E*. Well, *faster* also spells *strafe* if you take some time and shuffle your tiles thoroughly enough.

Some of these 'switch-hitters', especially the longer ones, were listed in the chapter on seven-letter words. The ones following here are some common, shorter ones that may help your game:

ache, each

abets, beats, beast, baste, bates

aids, said, dias

ales, sale, seal

amen, name, mane, mean

arid, raid

aster, rates, stare, tares, tears

angel, angle, glean

ascot, coast

aside, ideas

ajar, raja

beard, bared, bread

below, bowel, elbow

brief, fiber, fibre

browse, bowers

bleats, stable, tables

crapes, recaps, spacer, pacers, capers, scrape

cause, sauce

chaste, cheats, scathe

cheater, teacher

cited, edict

coax, coxa

corset, sector

crisp, scrip

cartel, claret

coins, icons, scion, sonic

dare, dear, read

daze, adze

dealer, leader, redeal

detail, dilate, tailed

drapes, parsed, spader, spared, spread

denied, indeed

dale, deal, lade, lead

diet, edit, tide, tied

earth, heart, hater

east, eats, seat, seta

emit, mite, item, time

ether, there, three

fares, fears, safer

filed, field, flied

filer, flier, rifle, lifer

finger, fringe

faster, strafe

girth, right

granite, tearing

groan, organ

glare, large, regal, lager

hares, hears, share, shear

hewn, when

horse, hoser, shore

hinge, neigh

inks, skin, kins, sink

itself, stifle, filets

inert, inter, niter, nitre, trine

jar, raj

jaunt, junta

kale, leak

kail, kali

laces, scale

lame, male, meal

leap, pale, peal, plea

limes, miles, smile, slime

lose, sloe, sole

lilts, still

mate, meat, team, tame

meteor, remote

notes, onset, seton, stone, tones

night, thing

ought, tough

orts, rots, sort, tors

parts, strap, traps, sprat

pines, spine, snipe

paws, swap, wasp

pares, pears, reaps, rapes, spare

pest, pets, step

paste, spate, pates, tapes

pores, poser, prose, ropes, spore

quote, toque

quiet, quite

rats, tars, star

respect, spectre, sceptre, scepter

reserve, reverse

saint, satin, stain

sheet, these

skate, stake, steak, takes

tires, tries, rites

tens, nets, sent

torque, roquet

unite, untie

use, sue

unhat, haunt

veal, vale

vase, save

vee, eve

when, hewn

wont, town

weld, lewd

wards, sward, draws

wider, weird

went, newt

yard, dray

yak, kay

20 Plurals

Some memorable arguments have erupted at my Scrabble table – as I'm sure they have at yours – by unusual attempts to transform words already on the board. On occasions, our games have stalled for interminable periods while wrangling went on over somebody's attempt to change a verb into a noun – like extending the word *exile* into *exiler* or *braid* into *braider*.

Both those examples, incidentally, are legal, and making nouns out of verbs is a field worth tilling. A nailer is one who nails, a hammerer is one who hammers, and if a cutter is one who cuts, then equally justifiable is a sawer for one who saws or a hacker for one who hacks.

But the longest, most vociferous, and most intense arguments I have found have usually concerned the pluralization of words. When can you add an *S* or *ES* to an existing word and legally pluralize it? The answer, if it is a noun, is: almost always.

There are some people, including lexicographers, who believe that any word in the language can be pluralized. For example, the word *pink* is an adjective, yet it can be used as a noun and used in a sentence like this – 'The house painter came with a selection of paint samples. He had four varieties of brown, five pinks, three reds, and a yellow.'

The word *if* is a conjunction, but it can be pluralized 'without any ifs or buts'. Patrick Barrett, an American lexicographer, pluralized *if* for me in another context: 'I have checked the above page and find six ifs in it.' Barrett also acknowledges the argument that, possibly, all words can be pluralized, but said, 'That really opens a can of worms.'

To me the question of when is a plural not a plural will always be known as 'the great veal debate'. Two friends, who shall remain nameless, were locked in a tight game and Player 1 put down the word *veal*. Player 2 added an *S* to make it *veals*, grabbing a triple-word score bonus plus the lead. The word was challenged, and the challenge triggered an argument that has simmered ever since.

Player 1 was right. The word *veals*, plural of *veal*, was not in the dictionary. But then nouns that take standard plural forms – an *S* or an *ES* – are never spelled out in dictionaries for space reasons.

Oxford doesn't spell it out as clearly, but Webster's, in its general rules on dictionary interpretation, supported Player 2. On the subject of plurals it said: 'The plurals of English nouns are regularly formed in writing by the suffixation of the letter *S* (hat–hats) or the letters *ES* (cross–crosses).'

Webster's next spelled out how plurals were pronounced and then said: '. . . although there are many exceptions to be noted, this regularity is so dominant that in theory all English nouns may be said to be capable of an analogical plural in the letters -*s* or -*es* and in practice little hesitation in so forming a new or unknown plural should be felt.'

Back to the word *veals*. According to Webster's, *veal* is a noun meaning 'a small calf'. It is also the flesh of a calf from a few days to 12 to 14 weeks old. It is also a verb – to veal – meaning 'to kill or dress a calf for veal'. Therefore, *veal* (the flesh) cannot be pluralized, but *veal* (the beast) can.

The discussion between the two players in this story led to questions over whether, if veal can be pluralized, you can have *beefs* and *porks*. In the case of beefs, the answer is 'Yes' with a qualification. The plural of *beef* (meaning 'an adult cow, steer or bull') is *beeves*. When *beef* means a complaint, then the plural is *beefs*.

Beef, the flesh, like *veal*, the flesh, is already pluralized. And so is pork. The only way *pork* can be pluralized is when it's a porker, and there is enough meat in that for continuing the argument.

I mention this at length because it is indicative of the type of argument that crops up again and again. There are three things to remember:

1 Most nouns can take an *S* or *ES* as a plural and, as Webster's puts it, you should show 'little hesitation' in doing so even if the plural is 'new and unusual'.

2 Just because a plural is not in the dictionary does not mean it is illegal. If the word *dog* is there, but the word *dogs* is not, there is no logic in demanding that *veals* should be.

3 If the pluralization is extraordinary (for example, *beeves*), it will be listed the same way that *mouse* and *mice* are or *deer* and *deer*.

Index